TOXIC RELATIONSHIP

HEALING YOUR HEART AND RECOVERING YOURSELF FROM AN EMOTIONALLY ABUSIVE RELATIONSHIP WITH TOXIC PEOPLE. STOP NARCISSISTIC ABUSE AND MANIPULATION.

A.P. COLLINS

© **Copyright 2019 - All rights reserved.**

The content contained within this book may not be reproduced, duplicated, or transmitted without direct written permission from the author or the publisher.

Under no circumstances will any blame or legal responsibility be held against the publisher, or author, for any damages, reparation, or monetary loss due to the information contained within this book. Either directly or indirectly.

Legal Notice:

This book is copyright protected. This book is only for personal use. You cannot amend, distribute, sell, use, quote or paraphrase any part, or the content within this book, without the consent of the author or publisher.

Disclaimer Notice:

Please note the information contained within this document is for educational and entertainment purposes only. All effort has been executed to present accurate, up to date, and reliable, complete information. No warranties of any kind are declared or implied. Readers acknowledge that the author is not engaging in the rendering of legal, financial, medical, or professional advice. The content within this book has been derived from various sources. Please consult a licensed professional before attempting any techniques outlined in this book.

By reading this document, the reader agrees that under no circumstances is the author responsible for any losses, direct or indirect, which are incurred as a result of the use of the information contained within this document, including, but not limited to, — errors, omissions, or inaccuracies.

TABLE OF CONTENTS

INTRODUCTION	7
CHAPTER 1: WHAT IS A TOXIC RELATIONSHIP?	**10**
Types of Toxic Relationships	10
The Consequences of a Toxic Relationship	18
The Effect of Toxic Relationships on Your Health	23
CHAPTER 2: DIFFERENCE BETWEEN A HEALTHY RELATIONSHIP AND HARMFUL RELATIONSHIP	**27**
What Exactly Is a Healthy Relationship?	27
Benefits Associated with a Healthy Relationship	36
What Are Addictive Relationships	39
The Psychology Behind Addictive Relationships	41
The Dangers Associated with Harmfully Addictive Relationships	43
Are There Signs and Symptoms of an Unhealthy Relationship?	45
Ways to Avoid Being Excessively Addicted to A Relationship	47
Differences Observed in Healthy and Unhealthy Relationships	48
CHAPTER 3: HARMFUL BEHAVIORS THAT MAKE A RELATIONSHIP UNHEALTHY	**54**
CHAPTER 4: TYPES OF PEOPLE MOST LIKELY TO FALL INTO A TOXIC RELATIONSHIP	**58**

CHAPTER 5: HOW TO RECOGNIZE A TOXIC RELATIONSHIP — 64

Why Is It Vital to Learn How to Recognize a Toxic Relationship? — 64

CHAPTER 6: WHY DO PEOPLE GET STUCK IN A TOXIC RELATIONSHIP? — 72

CHAPTER 7: HOW TO HELP THE PARTNER TO ENGAGE IN THE RELATIONSHIP MORE SERENELY — 81

Fix Your Relationship or Not? — 91

CHAPTER 8: RECOGNIZE WHEN NOTHING ELSE CAN BE DONE — 93

CHAPTER 9: SAY ENOUGH — 98

Knowing When to Say Enough and Walk Away — 99

CHAPTER 10: TIPS FOR GETTING OUT OF A TOXIC RELATIONSHIP — 107

Things You Should Know About Leaving a Toxic Relationship — 108

Leaving a Toxic Relationship — 113

CHAPTER 11: WHY DOES GETTING OVER AN UNHEALTHY RELATIONSHIP SEEM HARD? — 124

CHAPTER 12: HOW TO RECOVER FROM A TOXIC RELATIONSHIP — 130

CONCLUSION **135**

References 136

Introduction

Only those who have been in a toxic relationship can explain the level of pain, frustration, and emotional abuse that comes with it. However, individuals who have never experienced a toxic relationship before can prepare themselves, so they don't find themselves in one. Many victims in toxic relationships experience constant emotional abuse, which wears on their self-esteem down the line. In worse situations, this abuse becomes physical. They also experience gaslighting, manipulation, name-calling, financial and mental abuse and more. These are the universal tools of the toxic partner.

Many victims with toxic partners get abused to the extent that abuse becomes a norm for them. Their toxic partners break them down in every manner until they become a shadow of their former selves. Now, as a result of the abuse the victims go through, many of them are conditioned to believe they can't find happiness anywhere else. They believe this is the best they can get and that they are the cause of every treatment and problem they are facing in the relationship. As a result of this, many of these victims never get the zeal, desire, or courage to leave. The absence of a willingness to leave puts them in a much tougher situation; the toxic partners use the victims until they are no longer useful, then dump them. This leaves the victim alone to face all of the torture they have suffered during the relationship. For many people, recovery is possible, so long as they are ready to utilize the needed effort and time involved in the process. In worse situations, the damage is much more severe, and the victims may suffer the effects in various areas of their lives, including the way they react with others. Some victims never find love again and remain a shadow of their former selves.

Well, while this is the way it goes for a lot of the victims, it does not have to be the situation for you. If you are dealing with a toxic relationship presently, then you have taken a significant first step by purchasing this book. You still have ample time to escape from the clutches of your abuser. And the information you will find in this book can be of help.

In this book, you will find out what toxic relationships are. You will also learn the major reasons people remain in toxic relationships and how you can tell if your relationship is toxic. You will also learn how to get out of the toxic relationship and make a clean break for it, so that you can begin your life anew.

With this book, you will start the process of developing the life of your dreams, free from the negatives of a toxic relationship. Even if you are not in a toxic relationship, this book can show you the signs to watch out for, or how to help someone you know. To make things less complicated, this book is categorized into four sections. These include:

- **Section 1**: Covers all of the basics you of a toxic relationship, healthy and unhealthy addiction, and harmful behaviors that make a relationship toxic

- **Section 2**: Shows why individuals get stuck in a relationship

- **Section 3**: Explores how to help your partner grow a better relationship, understand when there is nothing left for you to do, and when to say enough is enough.

- **Section 4**: Delves into the various tips you will need to get out of a toxic relationship.

Now, let's take this journey to get free from the shackles of toxicity and help you live the life you truly desire.

Chapter 1: What Is a Toxic Relationship?

A toxic relationship hurts your dignity, your well-being, and your perception of yourself and the world. As toxic people go through life, they leave behind streams of broken relationships, broken individuals, and broken hearts. There are many individuals trapped in toxic relationships who do not even know they are in one. For many others, they know what kind of relationship they're in, but stay with the belief that things will get better along the line; sadly, it never does.

However, many unhealthy or toxic relationships do not start that way, and the person you met didn't seem toxic. There are times when relationships begin on an excellent note. However, some factors tend to arise, which may change even good people in relationships and over time, they change the relationship into a toxic one. Some of these factors include negative pasts, negative emotions, and desires which do not get met over a specific period. All of these tend to pile up and result in what we know as a toxic or unhealthy relationship. In most instances, this takes place in a flash, and even very emotionally stable people are affected too. There are numerous kinds of toxic relationships, and we will be looking into a few of them below.

Types of Toxic Relationships

There are some situations that breed toxic relationships. They include:

- When a person gets into a relationship with an individual who has an entirely different lifestyle from theirs which does not align in any way.

- When a person gets into a relationship with an individual that has a lousy personality.

Although there are various types of toxic partners in existence, they all end up in specific kinds of toxic relationships. In this section, we will be looking into these types of relationships.

Relationships with Domineering Partners

In these kinds of relationships, the controlling partner may want to influence every activity the other is engaged in. They do this even if they have to use aggression to determine what the other partner is doing.

If you are in a relationship where your partner needs to give you approval before you take a step, then it might be a problem. Relationships are about two people, and even in healthy relationships, it is fine to see what your partner thinks before you take a major step. However, when you are scared of doing the simplest things because your partner has to give you approval, then you could be in a toxic relationship and might need to get out as fast as you can.

Relationships with Jealous Partners

These sorts of partners always get incredibly jealous when their significant other spends time with other people. When this happens, the jealous one tends to believe their partner has some kind of sexual relationship with these other people. The same applies even when their partner has friendly banter with a friend. Everyone gets jealous in relationships; however, when it is done excessively, then the relationship becomes an unhealthy one.

Relationships with Partners Who Constantly Bring You Down

Always avoid a partner that tells you, "I told you so." These kinds of partners do not help you out when something goes wrong. They would instead make it look like you have no idea what you are doing, rather than help you out. Such people probably have issues they are not talking about or simply enjoy it when they make people around them feel less important.

Relationships with Partners That Cheat

Some people cannot be in a relationship without cheating as they enjoy the feeling that comes with it. If you have seen your partner cheating on you numerous times, you might not be able to change the situation. If you are with a partner that has no respect for you or a partner that does not think you are an important person, cheating will be the order of the day. This is a toxic relationship that nobody should ever find themselves stuck in.

Relationships with Negative Thinking Partners

Negative thoughts are bad for anyone as they have a way of interfering with your life. For this reason, being in a relationship with partners who are always thinking negatively is one of the most toxic relationships you can experience.

These kinds of partners believe that there is no good in life. They never see life in a positive light. They are either always speaking about a bad day they had or a terrible experience with someone. These sorts of individuals generally do not seem happy with life, and their nagging makes it draining for anyone to stay around them. This includes their partners too. Everyone has some complaints about life, and it is okay if done in little doses. However, if you have a partner who is always complaining about their life in excessive amounts, that partner might end up being a toxic partner.

Spending time with this sort of person will make you start feeling unhappy, and soon, you will become just like them. If you have to spend time around an individual that is extremely negative and complains too much, it can make you enjoy life less. You must spend time with people that see the light at the end of the tunnel and a glimmer of hope in the worst of situations. These kinds of people will help you improve your own outlook.

Relationships with Untruthful Partners

Some people always seem to find themselves lying. They just can't seem to resist the urge, even when it is not needed. They lie without remorse to their partners and are not bothered since there is no proof of the lie. When you find yourself in a relationship with a lying lover, frustration and insecurity will set in. You might even start feeling paranoid about your perception of the truth. All of these feelings build up, turning the relationship into one which is toxic.

These kinds of partners consistently make you believe something that is not true through manipulation. They enjoy using their words to control you and mess with your mind. They can be so conniving that you won't even know what is going on.

If you are in a relationship with a partner that has made manipulation and lying a habit, you might need to let them know you will not be a victim to their tricks. Life is not about games. If the person you are with wants to always play games, get them out of your world.

Relationships with Abusive Partners

Abuse does not only have to be physical. Sometimes it can be verbal or emotional. There are times when physical abuse and verbal abuse have the same level of effect on people. Abuse, in any form it comes, should not be condoned. If you have a partner that abuses you emotionally, verbally, or physically, this partner gets the power to dominate you. Staying too long in relationships like these can greatly reduce the self-esteem and happiness of a person down the road. For this reason, it is best to leave a relationship the instant you spot abuse.

Relationships with Overly Insecure Partners

If you are in a relationship with an individual and you need to travel to another city for some time, it is normal for insecurity to arise. It happens to everyone, and the situation worsens when either partner has a job that needs him or her to spend time around good-looking members of the opposite sex.

However, this becomes worse when your partner is extremely insecure. If you must constantly reassure your partner that you only have eyes for them, then this could be a problem. It is best to nip this in the bud as soon as you can, or it will become problematic for you down the road.

Relationships with Difficult Partners

Some partners expect you to always give everything you have to the relationship. However, they do not put the same effort they expect you to give into the relationship. This type of partner constantly tries to make you do their bidding. They also try to make you feel lucky for having them as your partner. If you find yourself in a relationship such as this, you might end up feeling miserable because you will never be as good as they want. No matter how much you try.

Relationships with Partners Who are Always Throwing Blame

These are partners who always blame their significant other for their errors and pile up their frustrations on them. These kinds of partners might simply believe their frustrations should be put on their lovers. Partners that think this way will keep getting pissed at you for no reason. When your partner blames you for something you did not do, do not take it from them. If you do, it will become a norm, and you will find yourself in a total mess. The love you share might turn into hatred and change your relationship into a toxic one.

Relationships with Extreme Perfectionists

It's a fantastic thing to be dating someone that everyone considers a perfectionist. However, if you are in a relationship with someone that has an obsession about how they want things to go, you will end up being frustrated. People that are both perfectionists and obsessive are impossible to please. They will always find fault in things even when none exists.

These kinds of individuals will always pick out flaws. You might have a fantastic body, excellent communication skills, and be a wonderful cook; the kind of person everyone dreams of. But, when you are with a perfectionist, these things do not matter as you will always have flaws. A lot of times, individuals who are perfectionists have to do things by themselves, or it won't be good enough. This is one reason why it is impossible to please them.

Relationships with an Alcoholic Partner

While virtually everyone loves to drink wine and have a little alcohol when the weekend approaches, this is a lot different from always being drunk. If you have a partner who is always getting drunk, things might be more complicated than you think. Although there is a lot of fun associated with drinking with your partner, if you never really get to see your partner sober, there is a massive likelihood that nothing will come out of your relationship.

Relationships with Competitive Partners

Certain people enjoy competing. If there is no competition, they are not interested. They might genuinely love you and care for you, but they will always want to do better than you in everything. This involves games and other more severe life occurrences. When they lose, they need a form of care before they are themselves again. The worst part is, they enjoy when you make a wrong move because they want to be the ones to help make things right for you.

Relationships with Narcissistic Partners

A little narcissism is good. However, like other traits we have mentioned above, when narcissism is extreme, it can be very infuriating. Narcissistic partners are very shallow and materialistic. They might genuinely love you, but they will treat you like an item and not a person with equivalent value. This type of partner gets offended when you are not dressed your best while going out with them. They act like life is all about them. No one enjoys being treated like an item, and a relationship like this can do a lot of damage to your self-esteem and emotional well-being. Besides, narcissists are controlling and manipulative, all of which can make a relationship extremely toxic.

If you find yourself stuck with a toxic lover, you need to find a way of getting out of such a relationship. Getting out is necessary because it will be nearly impossible to make the relationship any better. This is regardless of how much energy you put into trying to make the relationship better. The only time a toxic relationship can change for the better is if the toxic person decides to be more accommodating all by themselves. Knowing this, let's delve into some of the repercussions of remaining in a toxic relationship.

The Consequences of a Toxic Relationship

There are lots of ways unhealthy relationships can affect you. You can begin losing every form of self-worth you possess if you spend a long time in a toxic relationship. You might suddenly start to discover that you have lost your identity and only see yourself the way your toxic partner sees you.

Depending on the number of years you spent in a toxic relationship, it can take a lot of time to heal from the wounds left from such a relationship. In some instances, you might need to go through therapy for many years before this damage can be remedied and your ego restored. There are many individuals that have severe, traumatic disorders simply because they spent so much time in a toxic relationship.

Feeling less important is not the only severe effect of being in an unhealthy relationship for a long time. Another negative impact is that it can become difficult to accept the love of other people that mean well. Whenever someone offers you sincere advice or a helping hand, you are cautious about them. This feeling of suspicion can cause you to be more unhappy in all of your relationships.

This is an assurance that you might miss all the opportunities to live a happy life. If you are in a toxic relationship, then you may feel like you play a role in the way you are treated. You are made to feel comfortable with being loved conditionally, being treated in the wrong way, or being rejected by the person you are in a relationship with. In your subconscious, you expect other people to treat you the same way. Due to this, it is difficult for you to receive love very easily and also to feel deserving of any form of acceptance and love. The more time you spend in a toxic relationship, the more damage you suffer. Furthermore, it will become more difficult to embrace the right type of relationship which comes with acceptance and love.

However, these are only a few of the consequences you face from a toxic relationship. In this section, we will be looking into some ways a toxic relationship has an impact on your life, even after it's ended.

Your Partner is All You Talk About Even in Their Absence

The effect of a toxic relationship is even more than a lot of people imagine. In the absence of a toxic partner, the ill effect of the relationship you have with them still stays in your mind. When they are not there, you spend a lot of time talking to family, friends, and other people around you about the toxicity your partner brings into the relationship. You find yourself constantly nagging about the level of toxicity they bring into the relationship.

Toxic Relationships Damage Your Self-Assurance and Self-Esteem

The relationships we find ourselves in have a major effect on what we think of ourselves. You can have a very healthy dose of self-confidence by simply spending good quality time with individuals that accept your personality, love you for your exceptionality, and enjoy your presence. When around the right people, you can be successful. Furthermore, you get to enjoy life a lot more. However, unhealthy relationships have the opposite effect. They break down your self-confidence, self-esteem, and poison your level of happiness.

Toxic Relationships Consumes Tons of Energy

In an unhealthy relationship, you find yourself in a long-distance race to always please your partner. You are always busy, even when you are not conscious of it. In some toxic relationships, you have to be careful about saying the wrong thing. You find yourself continuously making an effort to know what mood they are in before speaking because they could be upset by even the slightest mistake. When you are with them, your entire focus is on them. You never get any attention for yourself, as asking for this might seem like asking for too much. Even worse is the fact that you won't get any form of support. When in an unhealthy relationship for a long time, you run out of energy. The time spent in a toxic relationship can be likened to the time spent on a long journey in an uncomfortable bus.

You Are Not in Charge of Your Emotions When You Are with Them

Toxic partners have complete access to your emotions. Their personalities have a significant effect on you. Due to this, you are unable to control the way you feel. This is so serious that you might end up hurting those people you love, as well as those in your world because of how unstable your emotions have become. This is not a position you want to find yourself.

You Display Negative Behavior and Put Them at Fault

Each time you display behavior that you know is bad, you do not take the blame for it. Instead, you put the blame on the toxic person around you. This is not good for two reasons. The first is it stands as evidence of how much they have affected you up to the point you act the way they want you to. The second reason is that they have succeeded in making you believe they are in charge of the way you act. And both of these are bad for an individual.

You are Uncomfortable in Their Presence

It is impossible to feel relaxed around a toxic partner. This is just the way it is. So, to feel comfortable, you should end the relationship you have with this person as this is the only way you will feel any form of peace. When you have no inner peace, it is your instinct trying to let you know that something is off, and you need to free yourself.

They Lower Your Dignity

It is effortless for toxic people to make others feel less like themselves. You have to avoid giving them power. One way to get this done is by making sure they do not take advantage of your insecurities. It is crucial that you hold fast to every form of self-confidence you have. Regardless of what they say to you, you have to have a good level of self-belief.

You Start Exhibiting Toxic Behaviors towards Others

When around a toxic person, you are at the receiving end of a lot of toxicity, and at some point, the urge to let it all out will be overwhelming. The only way to feel a bit better is to pass on some of the toxicity to the next person. And you really can't be sure who will be at the receiving end of your toxicity. Without a doubt, this is not the type of life you want to live if you have any form of care for those in your world.

You Adopt Unhealthy Coping Mechanisms

Being in a toxic relationship can make you pick up lots of bad habits. You might start doing drugs, smoking, drinking, and even overeating all in a bid to deal with the frustration and stress you are feeling. While all these might help you cope, they are unhealthy and might remain a part of your life if you do not get out of a toxic relationship.

You Let Them Walk Over You

If you continue to remain in a toxic relationship, you will be giving a person with poisonous characteristics the opportunity to get whatever they want from you. They will abuse you in ways you cannot imagine. And this is where the issues begin. To avoid falling into this trap, you need to be extremely careful whenever you find yourself around a toxic person. If you are gullible, you will get into trouble. At all cost, you must avoid any games they try to play.

The Effect of Toxic Relationships on Your Health

When in a relationship, your health should benefit positively. However, if your partner causes you unnecessary stress and concern, your health might be severely affected. Like we have covered before, every relationship has its ups and downs. However, when more than half the time you spend with your partner is ruled by misunderstandings and toxicity, to the extent that it begins to have an impact on your daily life, then it's a problem. If you are not sure how a bad relationship can negatively impact your health, below are some ways it can.

It Can Make You Lose Weight

If you are dealing with issues in your relationship, it can lead to weight loss. When facing emotional problems, eating can also become an issue. The things you love to consume might start growing tasteless. Situations such as this can cause you to lose weight. Furthermore, this could lead to a loss in color or paleness since it will be challenging to care for yourself in the right way. If you cannot cope in a bad relationship, you might end up losing weight.

Increase in the Level of Stress

Dysfunctional relationships are always very stressful. If you do not feel happy being in a relationship with someone, you will find yourself going through a lot of stress, and this could have a toll on your health. This is because excessive stress results in issues like anxiety, depression, high blood pressure, heart attacks, personality disorders, and stroke among many others. All of these are not ideal for your overall well-being.

Insomnia

Going without the right amount of sleep for a reasonably long period can negatively affect your health. When we go through problems, we tend to think a lot about our issues. This also applies to when we are in a toxic relationship. The problem caused by the relationship results in your overthinking. Now, when you spend so much time thinking, you might find sleeping difficult, and a decline in your state of health might be next.

Bad Mood

Dysfunctional relationships always put people in bad moods. Bad moods occur quickly when one is not happy about a particular circumstance. If you find yourself in a toxic relationship, your mood will be gravely affected, ultimately having an adverse effect on your health.

Headaches

Being in a toxic relationship can lead to unending headaches. When in a dysfunctional relationship, lots of disagreements are bound to take place. Now, having to always argue with someone you love can cause you headaches and ultimately have a terrible effect on your state of health.

Depression

When one goes through emotional and mental pain for a prolonged period, it can lead to depression. Toxic relationships can affect one's mood negatively and lead to depression.

Excessive Consumption of Alcohol

When people have unending bad times as a result of toxic relationships, they might try to feel better by always drinking alcohol. Doing this can have a nasty effect on your health.

Heartache

Dysfunctional relationships sometimes bring about heartaches, which affect your health badly. If you always have heartache because of a toxic relationship, you might end up being affected by various ailments.

Chapter 2: Difference Between A Healthy Relationship and Harmful Relationship

It can be said that having a healthy, functioning relationship is one of the hallmarks of living a successful and healthy life. This is mostly down to how, as humans, we crave social interactions to make us feel alive. And while the movie industry and romantic novels might paint a portrait of what a perfect relationship is, there is no such thing as a perfect relationship in existence. However, there is such a thing as a healthy relationship which we will be looking into below.

What Exactly Is a Healthy Relationship?

The most pertinent characteristics of a healthy relationship are love, happiness, and joy, with love being the most integral of elements. It is within the very fabric of our makeup to positively relate with others in a manner that enhances our relationships. However, there are times when even the best intentions go awry. We end up introducing the wrong type of individuals into our lives, causing us to have interactions that can be categorized as unhealthy, fruitless, or detrimental.

Below are some of the features that can be associated with a healthy relationship.

Friendship

There are specific characteristics associated with a healthy relationship. When we enter the one that has these characteristics, we begin to view the other person as someone that can be a best friend. Our interactions become more than just one dimensional, to the extent that we can have intimate conversations, sharing whatever it is we have on our minds. A relationship like that enables us to pool our resources and discover solutions to issues that either affect us individually or as a partnership. It has been proven that relationships based on friendship tend to have more staying power than relationships built on other variables. This is down to the fact that not only is there love between both individuals, but they also genuinely enjoy engaging in fulfilling activities together.

It Gives You Joy

Think about your past interactions with others; do you happen to look fondly on those that made you happy or those that were fun? If so, you can rest assured that a healthy relationship is one that contains fun and laughter. You should have pleasant moments with the person you are in a relationship with. It can be simple things, such as sharing the same humor or cooking dinner. However, like all things in life, there should be a balance. If you head into a relationship expecting to be happy at all times, you can be sure that you have unhealthy expectations of that relationship. Your healthy relationship should be a mix of happy moments and frustrations. Remember that conflict is an integral part of human interaction and that doesn't change simply because you are in a loving relationship with someone. You are both individuals with specific values and beliefs, that might be contrary to one another. The key is to compromise and not let those differences overwhelm the naturally flowing joy and happiness you derive from being with that person. What it means is that the life that you have both created together is a significantly happy one, rather than a mostly negative one.

Effective Communication

Being able to communicate effectively is another trait associated with a healthy relationship, as you can express whatever it is you are feeling clearly. With this type of relationship, there is no room for burying anger or hurt. Both of you have the capability and environment to deal with any situation you are faced with an effective manner. On the other side of the coin, unhealthy relationships tend to lack this hallmark, and that makes it much easier to identify the type of relationship you are in. When you are in a healthy relationship, you discover that you and your partner both speak the same language when it comes to emotional, intellectual, and physical matters. This can be easily attributed to the fact that you both are allowed to clearly identify and effectively communicate your desires, griefs, needs, and expectations.

Supportiveness

When it comes to a healthy relationship, being able to support your partner and have that support be appreciated is a definite sign of a positive relationship. They have to understand that you have a life outside the relationship. It is essential that you both support each other's ambitions and goals.

Everything in life requires effort, and a relationship is no different. The two of you have to be willing to come together and pool your resources, be it emotional, financial, or physical, to help each other achieve your goals and develop new ideas. A healthy relationship should also be one where you love each other. Healthy relationships require you and your partner to exchange support, help, and advice which can be used to help you attain any goals you have in life.

There are certain givens and mandatory responsibilities associated with a healthy relationship. Being able to understand each other without any masks or pretense as well as being able to support your friends, family, lifestyle, ambitions, and goals are essential.

Reliability and Trust

An explicit identifier of an unhealthy relationship is the absence of trust. A healthy relationship has to have trust. It is required, as you have to be able to trust in your partner, rely on them, and believe that they also are able to trust in you and depend on you. When in a relationship with someone, it is essential that you both give each other reasons to be truthful.

Being dependable is another aspect of trust in a healthy relationship. It is essential that you both can depend and rely on each other. Your word should be your bond. When this happens in a relationship, an environment in which trust and reliability exist is created. One partner can know the actions and words of another and what they signify. It is essential that every promise made is kept, as that helps reliability and trust grow in the relationship. This involves both partners remaining open to each other and not cheating.

Disagreements Are Normal, But You Forgive and, Most Importantly, Forget.

Conflict is a part of human social interaction. We see and experience it every day of our lives, from little disagreements to wars, it is a constant in every relationship. A healthy relationship is not immune to conflict. Simply because there is conflict does not mean you should break up your relationship. Conflict is an innate part of human interaction, so you should view it as an opportunity to get to know more about your partner, to understand them. This will help to foster harmony and love.

There is something peculiar about human interactions; it turns out that those closest to us, in terms of intimate relationships and love, are the ones that are likely to hurt us. Nobody is perfect. It is imperative to always remember this fact during your interactions as this will foster forgiveness of any wrongdoings, discrepancies, or mistakes made. To truly forgive means to ensure that the hurt and offense caused does not hold sway in your mind when interacting with your partner.

Comfortable Pace

While the world is a fast-paced one, certain things in life must flow at their own pace. A relationship is one of those things that has to dance to its tune. Most times, when we begin dating someone, there tends to be a desire to want to spend every waking moment with them. While there is nothing intrinsically wrong with feeling like this, as long as you both enjoy each other's company, you should ensure that you are not rushing things. Wanting to spend time with your significant other has to be something that you both want to do. It should not feel hurried or imbalanced in a healthy relationship. There should be no pressure to committing to each other, on sex, on meeting friends and family, on moving in together, or even beginning a family. The aforementioned are milestones that you both should be happy about when they are mentioned. It is imperative that there are no mixed feelings whatsoever.

Independence

While it might appear counter-intuitive, being independent is a strong identifier of a healthy relationship. When you and your partner have the freedom and space to show your true selves, then you can develop friendships outside of each other, while also still being able to acknowledge the fact that you are together and love each other. You don't have to know every intrinsic detail about your partner for you to love them.

Honesty and Respect

A healthy and fruitful interaction requires honesty, and a healthy relationship is no different. You should be able to be truthful with each other. Your communications should be free from any veiled messages or pretense. You both must be able to speak freely without being judged or worried about what their response is. While doing this, you should know that you have no control over how the other person feels about what you have said. However, when you are in a healthy relationship, your partner processes that information in a considerate manner.

Any relationship, regardless of what type it is, requires respect. When a relationship has respect, your partner values your opinions, beliefs, and any other things that make up your personality. It is essential for a partner in a healthy relationship to compliment you, support your dreams and ambitions. What they shouldn't do is to attempt to belittle you or overstep any boundaries you lay down.

Equality

Equality comes hand in hand with respect. Whereas respect ensures that you are not belittled and your boundaries are left intact by your partner, equality in a relationship provides you with an environment where you both can have an equal say. To achieve this, you both have to put the same amount of effort and commitment into the relationship. When this is done, you avoid the notion that one partner is subject to the whims and machinations of the other. A healthy relationship involves two individuals that come together to form a partnership. A healthy relationship is not one that consists of a leader and a follower; you should both work together when it comes to decision making. This is better than just one person having the responsibility of making decisions.

That being said, it is also vital that when a decision can't be made, both parties should be willing to make compromises. When this is done, you both can feel that your opinions and feelings are both respected and important.

Taking Responsibility

Respect begets equality and equality means that you have to take responsibility. Taking responsibility is not the purview of a single individual when it comes to a relationship. You both have to be responsible and accountable for your words and your actions.

Being in a healthy relationship means not choosing to blame each other for whatever mistake was made; instead, it is about accepting your faults and your actions when you do something wrong. Being able to genuinely apologize for any errors you make is a sign of a healthy relationship. Neither of you should be irresponsible to the point of taking things out on each other or paying each other back when you are angry. Another aspect of taking responsibility is to be able to come together to affect change in your relationship positively.

Loyalty

What is loyalty when it comes to a healthy relationship? Loyalty is what your partner exudes to show that he or she can be relied upon. This portrayal is one that should inspire confidence in you. A way your partner shows this is by being faithful and respectful. They should also be able to back you up, protect your secrets, and support you by providing a united front against outside influences. You should be able to find common ground. Most people believe that a healthy relationship requires loyalty tests; however, that just simply points to a lack of trust, which is a sign of an unhealthy relationship. It is imperative that you both understand that you are loyal to each other and no one else. One thing to remember is that we as humans are not infallible, so there will be points where mistakes will happen. However, these mistakes do not negate the fact that loyalty is pertinent to a healthy relationship. If you find yourself continually thinking otherwise, then it is a negative sign that your relationship might not be one that is healthy.

You Like Your Partner and Yourself

It might seem like a no brainer that you have to like the person you get into a relationship with; however, one thing you should never base your relationship on is the possibility of it getting better. Most people believe that if something beautiful was to happen to them, their relationship would automatically become the best it has ever been. This is why most people go on vacations in a bid to save their relationship or even decide to start a family. This is an exercise in futility. You have to fully understand that there is no such thing as a perfect human, so there will never be anything called a perfect relationship. You both have to value and accept each other as you are, rather than who you could be down the line.

You Are Both Kind to Each Other

Showing love, appreciation, consideration, and empathy to someone you care about is all part of being in a healthy relationship. One thing you should not do is place the priorities of strangers or people you have a mere association with, over that of your partners. If you find yourself doing so, it could be time to reset what your priorities are.

Benefits Associated with a Healthy Relationship

One thing that everyone should do once in a while is to take stock of the relationships in their life. This process should be used to discover what sort of relationship you have with others. You are likely to get a mixed bag of results, as some relationships are great and healthy, and there are some that are not. When dealing with an unhealthy relationship, it can be quite difficult to confront an issue that happens within the confines of that relationship, whereas in a healthy relationship, there exists an environment where you can face any issues you might have head-on.

This, as well as many other reasons, shows why it is beneficial for you to ensure that all your relationships are healthy. The term relationships, in this regard, encompass more than just romantic relationships. It involves relationships with family, colleagues, and friends. As social animals, every relationship we have influences every aspect of our lives. Knowing this, below are a few of the benefits you stand to gain from a healthy relationship.

A Healthy Relationship Can Help You Reach Your Goals

Being goal-oriented requires you to be motivated. To some, motivation is second nature; to others, it requires a little more forethought. A healthy relationship enables you to gain an additional source of motivation. This is possible due to the fact that when you are in a relationship with someone, you look to share your dreams, aspirations, and goals with them. You do this with the belief that they will offer their support to you. This support comes in different forms, and they might decide to actively help you reach your goals. The saying, "A problem shared is a problem halved", comes to mind. For example, by merely telling those around you that you would like to become healthier, they could decide to support you by ensuring the food choices you make are healthy. If you were to pick up an artisan trade, your friends and loved ones could assist you by being your very first customers and even putting the word out there about your skills. Goals appear easier to attain once you have this type of support in your corner.

You Have Better Social Time

Being around people is as natural as breathing. It is an innate desire as eating is. We are naturally social creatures. Choosing to engage in healthy interactions means spending time with people that you enjoy. Healthy relationships act as a barrier to being lonely or feeling terrible about yourself. They enable you to have a source of support when you need it and an ear to let out your feelings when required.

You Gain Access to Opportunities

There is some truth in the statement that opportunity is all about who you know. Opportunity comes to us all in numerous ways; it could be by being in the right place at the right time, through connections, or with the influence of a friend or a beloved family member. The moment you become involved in a healthy relationship with someone, you discover that they want nothing more than to see you become successful. This drive to see you become the best version of yourself includes them placing whatever resources they have at your disposal to ensure that you attain your goal. While the main reason you enter relationships should not be to take advantage of the opportunities that others present to you, it does clearly show why nobody should be taken for granted in your life. It does not matter if they are family, friends, or colleagues; your next opportunity could come from any of those relationships.

Now that you know what healthy relationships and addictions are, let's explore harmful addictive relationships.

What Are Addictive Relationships

Perhaps you have taken an appraisal of the relationship, you have knowledge of what a healthy relationship is, and you have categorized the relationships in your life, but some relationships are quite difficult to quantify. If you experience feelings such as emptiness, sadness, incompleteness, and despair in any of your relationships, it is safe to say that the relationship is an unhealthy or addictive, one.

Before speaking about it, we must first determine what an addictive relationship is. When one partner shows obsessive attention to the other, with little regard or attention for themselves, that relationship can be termed an addiction. These sorts of relationships are characterized by one individual's desire to connect and remain connected to their partner. This type of obsession manifests itself by making the individual in question understand that while the relationship might be unhealthy for them, they, for some reason, are unable to leave.

Individuals that are involved in addictive relationships tend to daydream and obsessively consider their partner. This overwhelming desire to think of their partner could cause them to have unrealistic hopes in their partner. This translates to giving an undue amount of their time and energy towards them. Typically, in a relationship, both partners create boundaries early on that help demarcate what is healthy and what isn't. These boundaries tend to erode in an addictive relationship. This is expressed by an individual willingly choosing to do anything or give anything up to ensure the survival of that relationship. It isn't just boundaries that become eroded in this situation; confidence can also be negatively influenced. An addictive relationship has the power to stop those in it from trying to be better in their personal life or to attain the highest positions in their professional lives.

It is easy for an outsider to logically ask those participating in an unhealthy relationship to leave. However, while these types of relationships can be painful, logic and rationality tend to be of no use when those in the relationship discover that they are unable to leave. Finding out that the relationship you are in is a harmfully addictive and unhealthy one is never the tricky part. The difficult part is trying to reconcile the need to leave for your self-preservation with the stronger, intense piece of you that either feels helpless on the topic of leaving or chooses not to do anything about it.

The Psychology Behind Addictive Relationships

One thing to be clear about when discussing harmfully addictive relationships is that the individuals involved do not set out with the intent to become addicted to love. They seek relationships with the very best of intentions. Everybody wants to be in a relationship that is healthy and happy. That being said, there is always an underlying battle with intimacy under that good intention. Addiction, regardless of it being of sex or love, typically stems from a feeling of insecurity. This manifests as an ulterior motive. There are numerous reasons for their insecurity, with the major one being the fact that the individual's family life could be one full of dysfunction. This dysfunction then causes individuals to search for a love object as a way to put paid to any matters of childhood that were unfinished. While a dysfunctional childhood relationship can be blamed, it isn't always the relationship that individual had with their parents that requires repeating. At times, the unresolved relationship in question could be one with any family member. This is a cycle that is bound to continually happen in whatever relationship that individual enters unless they can resolve this by mourning their childhood losses and start acknowledging their feelings. When this is done, that individual becomes able to select relationships that are much more positive.

For individuals with such tendencies who are looking to steer clear from addictive relationships, it is best to take the time out to know your prospective partner. This is an essential step to take before becoming romantically or sexually involved with one another. It has been proven that by allowing yourself to fall in love right after meeting someone, you allow your vision to become blurred. Having blurry vision increases the likelihood of you attaching yourself to any individual that exhibits an unhealthy, yet familiar pattern.

It is necessary for individuals that are addicted to love to become reacquainted with reality. A hallmark sign of potential addiction is an individual having intense fantasies in which their love interest can fulfill their dreams and make them happy. Another behavior these sorts of individuals are prone to is the desire to project their feelings onto individuals that they aren't too well acquainted with. The result of these emotions is a chemical high, which makes them feel good. While they feel good, these desires are not based in reality, nor are they factual because they do not know the object of their fanciful affection. This type of information is only gained by spending time with that person and experiencing them. The process by which addictive relationships function is by creating fanciful highs during the process of pairing. Whereas a healthy relationship grows and starts to become settled as time goes on, an addictive one never achieves equilibrium. An addictive relationship is sudden love, hopes, and fantasies, with no room for slow growth, causing it to burn out faster. Individuals in these types of relationships discover that they struggle to settle any natural differences that might occur when two people come together. In a healthy relationship, these difficulties are all part and parcel of getting to know one another. As stated earlier, a relationship is unable to succeed unless there is honesty in it; an addictive relationship bucks the trend as it is a relationship without honesty. The truth becomes so much a foreign concept in a relationship like this that any underlying dynamics are either ignored or faked. This can translate to the relationship lacking real intimacy.

Real intimacy can be defined as the capability of and having the environment to be able to freely speak on any matter that is risky or causes vulnerability. In its true essence, true intimacy eschews deflecting or apportioning blame as methods to evade being responsible.

It can be said that individuals who become addicted to relations have experienced childhood trauma. Trauma, in this sense, is the fact that they discovered frequently enough that it was better to keep one's real identity, thoughts and beliefs safe away when interacting with others. This decision was derived as a coping mechanism to ensure that their true essence was preserved, and they were unable to suffer disappointment. This caused them to have detached feelings. Coping mechanisms as such bring in toxic dynamics when perpetuated in adult relationships.

The Dangers Associated with Harmfully Addictive Relationships

Before being able to fix any issue, you are involved in, you must first recognize and acknowledge the dangers associated with them. It is no different from an addictive relationship. You have to be able to understand what risks an addictive relationship poses to you. You should also be able to recognize any addictive traits you might have that causes you to become intertwined with or attracted to addictive relationships. As with a healthy relationship, the feelings associated with addictive relationships might appear to be genuine fondness or deep attachment. This type of feeling, however, is prone to creating numerous adverse effects like alcoholism or drug addiction.

A harmfully addictive relationship is one that is unbalanced. This is manifested in one individual being wholly dependent on their partner. What this means is that any thoughts, decisions, or plans they make, have to be run by their partner. This does not happen because their partner requested it; instead, it happens due to the fact that they believe that it is essential for the wellbeing of the relationship if their partner is kept abreast of every decision they make. This process of overdependence causes the individual in question not only to lose their identity, but it could also cost them their future, as their decision making becomes severely hampered. It is one thing to have and be in an unhealthy relationship; it is also another to have that relationship transform into one that is controlling and overbearing. This transformation happens when the non-obsessive partner discovers the power given to them by the other individual. This loss of balance can significantly strain the relationship and also have the same effect on the obsessive individual without power.

A major point here is that addictions in a relationship are not the source of love. While it has the ability to mimic it, it isn't love. It is merely an addiction. A healthy relationship involves two individuals that are happy with each other, their personalities, their dreams and aspirations, and their entire beings. An addiction sullies that and causes an individual to not fall in love with who their partner is, but rather the idea and feeling of being connected to an ambiguous person. It is within this state that judgments begin to go awry, causing them to stay clear of logic and remain in a relationship or situation that ultimately is not for them. The result of a harmfully addictive relationship, regardless of its participants, is sadness and hurt.

Are There Signs and Symptoms of an Unhealthy Relationship?

Human nature and interactions are something that can never be set in stone. They are fluid and continuously change as the days go by. Relationships, being the result of these interactions, are also subject to the same ideal. This is why all relationships at one point or another show a couple of the traits below. Because of this, it would be foolhardy to evaluate a relationship based on one or two instances of the following characteristics. What you should do is focus on how many times these traits appear, as unhealthy relationships are more likely to have these traits show up regularly, and individuals in such relationships tend to be under more pressure and stress. Not only is this type of tension hazardous to both parties, but it could also spread and permeate into other aspects of their lives.

When you are in a relationship that is unhealthy, you might:

- Place one individual before another, simply by either neglecting your partner or yourself.
- Feel pressured to become someone you're not for your partner

- Feel worried the moment you disagree with your partner

- Apply pressure on your partner to change who they are to suit you better

- Realize that you both have to state justifications for your actions. It could be explanations about where they go or who they see

- Realize that one partner is obligated to engage in sexual relations.

- Have no privacy and feel compelled to divulge every bit of information with their partner.

- Either your partner or you don't want to practice safe sex

- Realize that there are no fair settlements in your arguments

- Experience physical violence or yelling when an argument is ongoing

- Try to manipulate or control each other

- Attempt to police your behaviors and how you dress

- Not take the time to be in each other's company. That is, you and your partner never take any time to enjoy the company of one another alone. In a healthy relationship, there are moments you spend time with your partner and do nothing but enjoy his or her company. This is absent in unhealthy relationships.

- Not having any mutual friends. It could also be that there is a shortage of respect when it comes to family and friends on both sides.

- Realize that one partner tends to have greater control of any resources like money, food, car, home, and more
- Realize that the relationship is not one that is equal or fair

If you observe that some of these traits apply to a few of the relationships in your life, it doesn't mean that the relationship has to come to an end. By merely recognizing these traits and how they affect you, you can improve any negative parts of the relationships to ensure that both parties benefit equally.

Ways to Avoid Being Excessively Addicted to A Relationship

It does not matter if you already are in an addictive relationship, or you are concerned about slipping into one down the line, there are a couple of steps that you can use to ensure that harmful love addiction does not form. The following steps should be followed to avoid any opportunity of marital codependency forming:

- You have to understand and value yourself. You should not let anyone make you dependent on them
- You should discover what it is that makes you happy when you are in a relationship and work to get that

- If you just left an addictive relationship, it is vital to allow some time to pass before inviting anyone else in so you can heal

- It is essential that you acknowledge and work on any struggles from your past that negatively influence you currently

- Recognize what an addictive relationship is at the initial stages and look to get help when formulating healthy boundaries

- Discover ways to be apart while still being in a relationship. This could be with differing friend groups or varying activities

- Develop a system of support which can be relied on. This support system should be separate from your partner.

Differences Observed in Healthy and Unhealthy Relationships

There are clearly numerous differences to be had between unhealthy and healthy relationships. These differences are so significant that it is challenging to pass off one relationship as another. When you can identify these differences, you gain an understanding of how healthy relationships function.

Make-believe as Opposed to Reality

Every healthy relationship is based on ideals and notions that are grounded in reality. In a healthy relationship, both parties are aware of their weaknesses and their strengths. There is an environment of trust and honesty, which means no partner has to hide anything from the other. This environment of trust and honesty is one that also functions both ways. There is no need to skirt around particular topics or issues. Both parties in a healthy relationship can come together to discover areas they are weak in. When an area is determined, the individual accepts that weakness and understands that their partner will never hold it against them. What their partner does is either move to help strengthen their partner or simply accommodate the weakness.

Unhealthy relationships, however, are based on fanciful ideas, and on notions of what could happen, rather than what is. This is a relationship that is rooted in fantasy. The focus in such relationships is on unrealistic elements, and this causes such a relationship to have a shallow existence as there is nothing rooted in reality to base the relationship on.

Finding Completion as Opposed to Completing

One stark difference between a healthy relationship and an unhealthy one is that a healthy relationship has participants that actively want to discover things about their partner. They relish the growth of their partner and are always willing to play their part to complete them. The difference in an unhealthy relationship is that rather than both parties focusing on how the relationship as a whole could grow and benefit, there is more of a selfish focus on completing the individual. An unhealthy relationship is the ideal breeding ground for codependency. This is done to the "me first" attitude that one or both parties carry in the relationship. It can also be where both parties are focused on just one individual.

Remarkably, there are quite a number of individuals that enter into a relationship with half the required effort, believing that the other individual in the relationship will make up for it. This is something that is never going to work. While healthy relationships are all about sacrifice and being there for one another, one thing that cannot be replicated by any person is individual effort. For a relationship to blossom, both parties must put in the same energy. Expecting the other person to make up for your lack of effort is something that can never work. It is an ideal example of an idea that is rooted in fantasy, as nobody can meet those expectations. When those expectations are not met, this causes the individual with half the effort to search for a substitute. This substitute is not always necessarily another relationship; sometimes, it is an addictive and dysfunctional behavior.

Fear as Opposed to Security

In a fast-paced world that is increasingly changing, it is normal for us to seek security in our everyday lives and relationships are no different. This couldn't be truer for individuals with childhoods that were extremely insecure. This past insecurity causes them to seek out relationships throughout their lives that allow them to be genuinely cared for. The truth is, there is a lot to life that is quite risky, and as humans, thanks to evolution, we attempt to negate that risk in any way we can. Forming a relationship with someone we believe cares about us and wants makes us feel safe can help us feel more secure. The moment we switch from attempting to exploit others for our security requirements to trying to meet the security demands of others, it is only at that moment that we discover a new dimension. Doing this enables us to concentrate on more than just our own needs. We assuage any fears that our partners might have by offering reassurance through our dependable behavior. In a healthy relationship, this reassurance and security goes both ways, with both people caring for each other. It is this type of love that offers absolute security and eradicates fear.

Defensiveness as Opposed to Vulnerability

As stated earlier, a healthy relationship is one that provides an environment for both parties to be fully vulnerable and open. Being able to be and feel vulnerable is a great feeling. It enables you to place your trust in your partner. You understand that in your time of need they will be there to catch you. This is a great feeling, and it is one that offers rewards as you are encouraged to become even freer. Being in a relationship that has this sort of environment enables you to discover who you are and also appreciate all the things you have in your life.

Conversely, when the relationship is one encompassed by fear, the opposite happens. It is necessary to begin putting up walls. This is because you believe that if you don't protect yourself, you are likely to be smothered, controlled, violated, or stripped of who you are.

Deception as opposed to Honesty

The bedrock of all healthy relationships, regardless of whether it's an intimate or platonic relationship, is honesty. For a relationship to be one that lasts long, it is essential for there to be an atmosphere of trust. Honesty is extremely integral to the entire relationship and everything that is done within it. This is because human interaction flourishes when there is an honest exchange of ideas and words. Deciding to tell little white lies in hopes of sparing pain that our honestly might cause to those we care about, can appear to be a noble cause. However, this is a slippery slope, and it does not take much for it graduate from telling little white lies to outright dishonesty. It does not take long before it becomes a habit, and when it is one, it can be quite a difficult habit to break. One of the ways to help eradicate it is to ensure that the dishonest person is always held accountable for their actions and words.

Resentment as Opposed to Forgiveness

There are tons of things to be said about forgiveness and the act of forgiving. Most people see it as an act that is done for the sake of someone else; however, it is an act done to one's self on behalf of others. As conflict is a natural part of human interaction, there are bound to be instances where one person crosses and wrongs the other. A healthy relationship acknowledges this fact and understands that it is all a part of growing together. When you choose to forgive your partner, you provide the relationship an opportunity to flourish. You let yourself overlook any past disappointments and hurt. Choosing not to forgive carries those disappointments and hurts around the relationship, burdening it. The sign of a healthy relationship involves someone being completely forgiven for making mistakes. There is no room for lording one person's mistake over them. It is a great feeling to relieve someone you care about from any mistakes they have made in the past. Doing so unencumbers the relationship, ensuring it can reach its full potential.

Victimization as Opposed to Friendship

In an ideal world, a relationship would be defined as two good friends becoming even greater friends. The most successful and most durable of relationships have embodied this notion, this feeling of true and real friendship. If you are in a relationship that is not founded on such principles, it can be said that your relationship is shallow and has a likelihood to be unhealthy.

Chapter 3: Harmful Behaviors That Make a Relationship Unhealthy

When you love someone with toxic behaviors, you may not be able to notice with ease. This is because your feelings make it even more challenging to spot. Furthermore, some relationships start healthy but later change into toxic ones without you even noticing. For this reason, you need to learn to spot the harmful behaviors that can transform a healthy relationship to one which is unhealthy. This way, you can correct yourself if you are the one exhibiting these behaviors or call out your partner if he or she is. In this chapter, we will be looking at some of the harmful practices you need to look out for in your relationship.

They Never Care About What you are Going Through

A toxic person has a reputation for always sharing their problems with you each time they have one, and they always expect you to be of help. They, however, do not give you any attention when you need them to solve a problem.

They Make Frustrating You a Habit

It is not a break from the norm for interpersonal relationships to have a bone of contention because of the different interests and opinions of those involved. But people with toxic attributes always seem to find a way to ensure you have negative feelings. They do this by either making you feel some guilt or making you angry. If you always go through some imbalance with your emotions whenever you are around someone, there is a considerable likelihood that this person is toxic.

They Are Always Ready to Discover Your Flaws

Everyone has a flaw or something imperfect. However, with the right person around, we can become better people and improve ourselves. But, If you have someone around you who is always ready to tell you your flaws without noticing the things you have accomplished, that person is toxic. Instead of trying to help you improve, this person keeps using your weaknesses to tear down your confidence and self-worth.

Your Feelings Are Not Important to Them

As individuals, we all have a bit of empathy. This is a vital attribute which allows us to consider others. However, toxic people lack this attribute. Instead, selfishness is a major attribute for them. This is one reason it is effortless for them to put other people under pressure all in a bid to get whatever it is they want. Toxic people are all about things that are in their favor and are not interested in making sacrifices of any kind. Due to this, they make use of various techniques in getting you to make moves that are contrary to your beliefs and values.

They Make You Have Doubts

It is not a bad thing to have people who let you know the flaws in your plans or decisions because then you can improve your plans. But certain people only notice risks and make you doubt your plans. These people are not precisely cautious. They are simply people that are not ready to get out of their comfort zone and want others to stay in their comfort zone also. Therefore, they have a reputation for coming up with uncertainties in projects that they are involved in. If your partner is exhibiting the sort of behavior that makes you forgo your dreams, then it is an extremely harmful behavior.

They Keep Crossing Boundaries

Toxic people have no regards for the rights of those around them. This is one reason they keep going over the line endlessly. It appears like they always carry out tests to see how much you can take. They keep getting into your space, taking your time and also want you to continually give them attention each time they request it. Failure to do things their way means they will manipulate you emotionally to make you feel some guilt.

They Do Not Like Change

In many instances, if we have to keep up with some relationships, change is one thing that has to occur. When two people are in a relationship, for things to work the way they should, the two people involved in the relationship will have to go through some changes. However, if one person is ready to change but the other is unwilling to, it is best to stay out of such relationship as the other party is not willing to put in any effort to make things go smoothly.

Chapter 4: Types of People Most Likely to Fall into A Toxic Relationship

Finally, you met someone who ticks all of your boxes in a relationship. At the start of the relationship, everything was fantastic. And you began to think, perhaps this is the perfect relationship, and everyone seems to think so too. Yes, there are a few hitches along the line, but to you, this is similar to other kinds of relationships. Or that is what you think. Suddenly, they begin to mistreat you, and you make up excuses for them because they apologized. However, of late, you realize that you have been doing more of the apologies.

The worst part is that you don't even know where you went wrong. But still, you apologize because it seems easier than arguing. Soon, things escalate, and you soon realize that you have started to suffer emotionally. Deep inside you, it is evident that this person is not right for you, but for some reason, you choose to stay because you remember the person they were. And you continue to suffer.

The above is the typical scenario for people that get stuck in toxic relationships. The truth is, that it is normal for a relationship to hit wrong turns, but the problem arises when it becomes excessive. Some individuals can spot these red flags and leave the relationship when they notice it cannot be saved. These kinds of individuals understand what a healthy relationship entails and can cut ties when it starts to change. Sometimes, they are even able to end the relationship on good terms with their partner even if it is heartbreaking for them.

However, some individuals do not know the appropriate moment to leave a relationship. These individuals tend to cling to the relationship, even if it is already dead. The relationship does not bring them any form of happiness, but they hold on anyway. So, what kind of people tend to do this? That is what we aim to elaborate in this chapter. Below, we will be looking at the people most likely to fall into toxic relationships.

People Unable to Experience Solitude

People who don't know how to deal with solitude tend to remain in a toxic relationship. These kinds of individuals are so scared of isolation that it tones down every other unhealthy behavior their partner throws their way. To this kind of partner, being in a relationship, even one which is toxic is better than dealing with solitude.

For this kind of person, it is possible to deal with this feeling. They need to learn to be happy with themselves. Learning to deal with solitude while managing to stay happy can help you deal with the fear of being lonely. The instant you can do this, you will never have to be stuck in a toxic relationship again.

People Who Fear They Will Never Find Someone Else

As humans, finding someone to spend the rest of your life with and share memories is natural. Besides, for many of us, this is a core objective in life. Sadly, this makes many people settle for less because of the fear of not being able to find someone else.

The idea of lowering your guard to start searching for another partner can be staggering. This is the case, particularly when you consider all of the stress involved in the search. So this makes people cling on to the person who is presently available, regardless of how toxic they are to our well-being.

If you are holding on to an unhealthy relationship for this reason; you need to understand that there is someone perfect for you out there. Yes, it might take a little time, but if you refuse to take the step and leave the toxic relationship now, you will never find them. There is someone out there who is very suitable for you and will ensure you are always happy.

People Who Are Afraid of Others' Judgment

When a relationship ends, there is a level of loss and shame that comes with it. Many people feel defeated because they were unable to make it work. When this feeling is at a basic level, it is perfectly normal. However, when this feeling becomes extremely excessive, then this is when it becomes a problem. Some individuals see a breakup as similar to failing a job selection test or losing a job. Sadly, when people have this widespread feeling of shame, it can result in things lasting longer than they are supposed to.

People who are extremely ashamed of breakups and don't want to deal with the repercussions of one, are likely to stay in toxic relationships. For these kinds of people, the thought of facing those around them and explaining why their relationships did not pan out is too much to bear. In the end, they choose to remain in the relationship even if it is not working out for them.

People with Low Self-Esteem

People who have low self-worth or self-esteem have a higher probability of remaining in an unhealthy relationship. They do not have the power to call their partners out when they are being mistreated; neither do they have the power to leave.

As stated by a research carried out by the Waterloo University; people with low self-esteem are likely to remain quiet when it has to do with problems in their relationship. This is because they are scared that the rejection that comes with it could end up making them less happy ("Intimate partners with low self-esteem stay in unhappy relationships", 2015).

People Who Are Afraid of Change

Having a consistent routine and structure in our daily lives can have a lot of impacts. For instance, imagine how awkward you would feel if the first thing you did each morning was to do some pushups. And then suddenly the for some reason, you had to break this pattern. Imagine how empty the rest of your day would feel if this happened?

Think of this feeling in a relationship. When you spend a lot of time growing and bonding with someone, you both develop patterns and routines together. Over time, your brain gets accustomed to the habits you have both built. In the event this kind of relationship ends, you immediately feel the full impact of breaking that pattern. It is the norm in every relationship, and many people learn to live with it even though it is a painful feeling.

However, some people are very scared of breaking their routines and would choose not to. For these people, not doing things they are used to doing with their partners is a worse feeling. Instead of leaving this sort of relationship and deal with the break in pattern that comes with it, they will prefer to stay in a toxic relationship.

If you are in this situation, all you need to do is take the first step. The instant you go past the first thanksgiving or event you both share, you will be able to live with the change.

People with Childhood Problems

Individuals who have faced some form of trauma in their childhood from those who were meant to care for them have a tendency to remain in toxic relationships. In worse scenarios, these individuals go out of their way to make these destructive relationships work. People like this search for others who fit with the identity of the individual responsible for traumatizing them in the past and hover around them.

The result of this is that they end up with individuals who are emotionally abusive, narcissists, or people who are not emotionally available. In other instances, they make a lot of effort to fix or save people they enter a relationship with. In their heads, these people know what they desire. However, they end up being unconsciously drawn down the traumatic road they are used to. When people around them try to warn them of the dangers of their choices, these kinds of people may choose their new partner over friends they have known for a while.

However, you can break out of patterns which lead you to continue an unhealthy relationship. Learn to spot the red flags and be ready to move on when you notice the familiar signs. Having covered this, the next chapter will be covering the signs of a toxic relationship so you can better protect yourself by leaving the relationship or calling out your partner to change.

Chapter 5: How to Recognize a Toxic Relationship

There are relationships we get into that offer us numerous benefits. They help us improve and ensure we are better than we were before the relationship. However, some relationships have the opposite effect. They make us lose our self-worth as individuals and change us into worse people than we were when we got into the relationship.

These sorts of partners tend to hurt you purposely or unknowingly until you begin to doubt everything. Many toxic individuals who could be your spouse, co-worker, or friend continue to manipulate you till you believe you are responsible for all the problems they are dealing with. These sorts of individuals deplete and drain all of your energy.

Regardless of where you find yourself, you do not want to be in a toxic relationship with anyone. For this reason, you need to learn to recognize a toxic relationship, and we will be teaching you how in this chapter. But first, why is it important to learn how to spot a toxic relationship?

Why Is It Vital to Learn How to Recognize a Toxic Relationship?

In relationships, the parties involved are expected to be of help to one another when things are not so rosy without having any expectation of a returned favor. You're supposed to help each other in times of need. When a lot of people hear the word "relationship," what comes to their minds is a romantic relationship involving two members of the opposite sex. Although very widespread, this is not precise. This is because any two individuals can be involved in a relationship, and toxic relationships do not have to be between people involved romantically.

Humans flourish when they have company and feel bad when alone. When one is in a toxic relationship, such a person might battle with inner conflicts which might result in depression, anxiety, or anger. It is vital that you can spot signs of a toxic relationship, as well as toxic individuals. This way, you can avoid unwanted emotional traumas. Below, we will be delving into a few signs of a toxic relationship.

You have Become Isolated

If you have started staying away from your friends and loved ones because of your relationship, then it is a red flag. If it seems your partner is discouraging you from spending time with people you love, suddenly your relationship has become toxic. This is a primary technique used by narcissists who have the aim of completely dominating you.

Isolation is usually not apparent. The toxic partner does it subtly via different tactics. These could range from taking charge of the events or activities the other partner takes part in, always calling to "check up" on them, or requesting that their partner stops other personal activities because their relationship takes priority.

Another strategy used by the toxic partner to isolate the victim is via financial abuse. Here, the toxic partner takes complete charge of how the other partner spends cash or earns it. A partner who uses this technique may request that you stop your job or get a new one because it is not giving you enough time to focus on your relationship. In the end, you may start to depend on the partner for financial assistance, which is their goal.

A healthy relationship consists of 2 mature individuals. As adults, you do not need to request permission from your partners when trying to do basic things. Compromise is essential in relationships, and it is vital to think of your partner when making massive life decisions, such as having to undergo extensive surgery or buy a new house. However, if it feels like you have to seek permission before doing minor things like spending time with friends or going to the store, or you appear to be uncomfortable when making fundamental decisions without your partner, it could show that there is something wrong and a clear sign you are in a toxic relationship.

Through the use of isolation as a means of cutting you off from your family and others around you, the toxic partner gets more control. Isolation can also be used in creating a vacuum in the relationship for the toxic partner to engage in other harmful and destructive behaviors. Eventually, victims may feel that they have no one to confide in about their experiences. This leaves the victim without a support system during perilous times.

If you observe all of these in your relationship, then it is a clear sign that you are dealing with a toxic relationship.

Asymmetric Relationship

Asymmetric relationships occur when one of the two partners in a romantic relationship has an excessively dominant role. In essence, one of the partners is more devoted to the relationship than the other partner.

Researchers grounded this concept on a theory established by sociologist Willard Waller. The theory was known as the "Principle of Least Interest." This theory connotes that the individual with a lower amount of interest in the relationship has a higher level of control. This is why many individuals urge themselves to act cool in social situations. It is also why many people take excess time in responding to texts even though they have an interest in the person (Stanley et al., 2018).

In a more recent study, researchers decided to try out this theory in romantic relationships. This was done to determine the kind of partners who keep the most control in relationships. Below are a few things they observed, which may indicate that you are in an asymmetric relationship (Stanley et al., 2018):

- Your partner believes that there are numerous fish in the sea.
- Your partner has issues getting attached and opening up to others.
- They have numerous exes.
- If your partner has cheated on you or does so continuously.

If you have observed that your partner does any or all of the following, then you may be dealing with an asymmetric relationship, which makes it a toxic one.

Other ways your relationship could be asymmetric include:

You are Obsessively Dependent

Codependency is categorized as a relationship where two individuals become so attached and invested in each other that they are no longer able to function separately. In this situation, the identity, happiness, and mood are determined by one of the partners. In these sort of relationships, one person has more dominance over the other. What's more, this individual gets a feeling of fulfillment from controlling the other partner and how they live. In this case, this is the toxic partner.

Dependence on someone you love and hope to spend the rest of your life with is not generally a bad thing. However, when you get obsessively dependent on your partner, who starts to show signs of control, this may be a problem. Being controlled by your partner and being excessively dependent on them don't go without one another. A toxic or controlling partner usually makes you dependent on them so you can help them satisfy their requirements. They may manipulate you until your entire life revolves around them, which gives them more control over you.

You need to remember that being excessively dependent on another individual is not due to love, but fear. When a toxic partner makes you responsible for them staying happy, their constant requirement to be validated begins to seem like an addiction. Your partner starts to control you, and it transforms into emotional dependency because you don't want to lose your partner. Being excessively dependent on your partner can lead you to totally let go of your identity to make your partner happy. Besides, your self-esteem may be centered on the relationship without your knowledge. If your relationship has started to feel this way, then it may have become a toxic one. If you are not sure about this, below are some of the general signs that can help you determine if your relationship is an emotionally dependent toxic relationship:

- You find it hard to make any decisions without your partner.

- You have trouble pointing out your feelings.

- You have low self-esteem and don't trust your judgment.

- You are scared of being abandoned and desire a constant need for approval

- You have problems expressing yourself in your relationship.

Individuals who are excessively dependent on others have a higher likelihood of transforming even healthy relationships into toxic ones. If you notice yourself portraying any of the symptoms listed above, then this is a major sign of a toxic relationship.

They Blackmail You

Emotional blackmail is an elaborate means of manipulation where individuals we are close to dish out threats to us because we failed to do their bidding. This is a prevalent strategy used by toxic partners. Many toxic partners who are apt at emotional blackmail understand the value we place on the relationships we have with them. They know your darkest secrets and know your weaknesses, which are typically not a bad thing in a healthy relationship. However, in the hands of a toxic partner, this can be very dangerous. If you observe that your partner is hurting and manipulating you as a means of punishing you, then it is a clear sign that you are in a toxic relationship.

There are many strategies used by the toxic partner to blackmail you emotionally. All of these are done to make you do their biddings. They include:

Capitalizing on your Fears

Fear is a feeling which keeps us safe from jeopardy. However, a toxic partner can take advantage of this feeling of fear to make you do their bidding. Below are the kinds of worries these toxic partners capitalize on to manipulate you:

- Fear of being abandoned
- Fear of getting others upset
- Fear of being abandoned

- Fear of confrontation

- Fear for your safety

Capitalizing on your Sense of Obligation

A toxic partner can make you feel obligated so they can do what they want. To achieve this, they use various strategies to make you feel bad about yourself if you don't carry out your obligations. For instance; if your partner requests that you do something you are uncomfortable with, and they remind you of all the times they went out of their way for you or tell you they would have done the same for you. Regardless of the way they go about it, you will feel a sense of duty to do their bidding, even if it is not your desire.

Guilt-Tripping you

Many toxic partners use your guilt to punish you. If you fail to do your obligations, they can use your guilt until you feel bad about yourself and do what they want.

If you have ever been blackmailed by your partner using any of the following methods, then you may be in a toxic relationship.

Chapter 6: Why Do People Get Stuck in A Toxic Relationship?

To people on the outside, a toxic relationship could be challenging to understand. Many individuals often wonder why those in these forms of relationships still remain, especially when it is clear that the relationship is toxic. Outsiders may try to inform the victims in a logical manner why they should get out of the relationship because it could result in a detriment to their health.

But the reasons why a person would decide to stay in a relationship which is unhealthy and damaging to their well-being are enormous. So, it is not something you can easily point out as an observer. That being said, in this chapter, we will be looking into some of the reasons why people get stuck in a toxic relationship. This way, you will better understand why people remain in one and understand if you have the same motives for staying in an unhealthy relationship too.

They Know Nothing Else

In some instances, individuals are unable to tell if they are tied up in a toxic relationship. This is especially the case if the individual has not been in a relationship beforehand, and this is the only way they believe a relationship should be. Sadly, many individuals are not taught how to grow a loving relationship properly, and this is the reason they end up in unhealthy ones. For many, the understanding of relationships they have is obtained from people around them, which may include their elders and peers. And in many cases, these role models don't even have healthy relationships of their own.

There are times when it is challenging to know if your relationship is toxic, especially if that relationship is the only one you know. Regrettably, nobody ever teaches you how to you can nurture a relationship with love. The earliest examples that most people get of relationships are through their parents and any elders we know. It requires self-education and intense effort to understand what exactly a healthy and loving relationship is. However, if you can't point out what a healthy relationship is or looks like, then you have a clear warning sign about your current relationships. You shouldn't feel bad about this. Instead, be willing to take the leap and learn about the traits of both a healthy and toxic relationship in the real world.

They Feel Undeserving

Low self-esteem and the belief that they don't deserve the best are some of the reasons why people stay in bad relationships. When you decide to stay in an unhealthy relationship, you're stopping yourself from experiencing a better and healthy relationship. Some people stay because they believe they deserve less, and also because of the benefits they derive from staying. Staying is a way of telling your partner that you deserve the treatment you are getting. However, when you leave, they'll understand that you're not ready to take whatever they throw at you. It's also a way of telling them that you have the right to choose what's best for you.

History Tends to Repeat Itself

People that are brought up in abusive homes view abuse as a norm, and as such, they do not feel they need to leave. They grew up without love for themselves, let alone loving others. These people always try to justify the negative actions of their abusive partners by overestimating their positive sides. As a result, leaving becomes hard and staying becomes the best option they have.

They Are Scared

Being scared is one of the leading determinants of remaining in a bad relationship or leaving one. People stay because they are scared of being judged, losing everything, being ridiculed, or being alone. They keep asking yourself questions like, "What will people say? How can I survive alone? How do I move on? How do I survive alone without the security and comfort that my partner provides?". They are scared of almost everything, and this makes leaving very difficult. People with these fears stay too long in bad relationships, and this has adverse effects on them.

False Understanding of Relationships and Love

Having a good understanding of love and healthy relationships will help you understand that love should come naturally. Some people believe love and healthy relationships require you to put in a lot of effort for it to work, but this isn't so. You don't have to be poorly treated, and any relationship that threatens the wellbeing of both you and your partner isn't healthy. Falling in love and being in a good relationship should not be what you fight for. Instead, this should come naturally.

They are Afraid of Hurting Their Partner

Humans, by nature, are social creatures. This is why many of us have empathy when dealing with others. We try to consider how people feel and how not to cause any harm to them. Sadly, for those in toxic relationships, this manner of empathy is usually taken advantage of by the abuser. Many people in bad relationships will put the needs of their partners first without caring about themselves. They care too much about their partner and will avoid hurting them without considering the amount of pain they've endured by being with their partner. Because they don't want to hurt their partner, they stay in the relationship. As a result of this, they keep pushing the breakup further back and fail to realize the immense level of pain they are putting themselves through.

They are Waiting for Things to Get Better

Some people stay in toxic relationships because they presume things are going to change. They may continuously believe that the present abusive status of their relationship is only for a while, and things will get better. However, this continues for days, months, or even years. With the hope that things will change for good, these sorts of individuals find excuses for their partner even under severe abuse. They make excuses that their partners are stressed, have a busy lifestyle, or are dealing with financial issues.

They allocate these as some of the reasons why their partner is abusive. They don't see their partner for who they are and believe they'll change as soon as they can overcome these things that stress them daily. As you stay longer in a relationship, you'll get to understand that rather than waiting for your partner to change, you should leave such a relationship.

They are Used to Pain

An interesting thing to note is that if you spend a sufficient amount of time doing something for so long, you will get used to it, and keep doing it. The same also applies if it is something that is supposed to be terrifying. This analogy can be used for unhealthy relationships.

The more time you spend in a bad relationship, the more you get used to the abusive nature of your partner. Pain is the norm, and you're used to every form of it. From emotional to physical abuse, constant degradation, and embarrassment, it doesn't hurt as it used to at the early stage of your relationship. You've also come to accept this with the belief that there are no better relationships out there. With this, you give up on finding happiness and a healthy relationship. This is a major reason why people remain in relationships even if it is unhealthy for them.

They Remain for the Sake of Their Children

Many parents would love to give their kids the best of everything in this world. In the course of preventing being divorced or separated from their kids, individuals in bad relationships will prefer to remain there. They also do this to avoid being blamed by their kids for not doing their best in ensuring the success of the relationship.

They are Being Manipulated

In some unhealthy relationships, there is usually a manipulative partner who takes advantage of the victim at every opportunity. These partners abuse their victims, and stylishly controls all aspects of their life. Many people stay in bad relationships because they're being manipulated to think they will regret ever leaving the relationship.

Abusive people usually ensure that they take you as far away as possible from people that'll provide support to you when you need it. If they don't do this, they'll ensure that you're isolated by finding faults in the people that love you and telling you that you're too good for them. Some partners also threaten to hurt you or themselves if you leave and as such, you have no option but to stay. These, among a host of other methods, are ways a toxic partner manipulates his or her victim into remaining in the relationship.

They have No Way to Leave

Many people are trapped in unhealthy relationships because they have no means of leaving. They may not be able to leave because they do not have anyone to help and encourage them. So, even if they feel like leaving on many occasions, they simply give up because of the uncertainty that comes with their being alone. They may always think about the happiness and peace that comes with leaving, but they can't simply leave because the strength, support, and courage is lacking.

Not Willing to Admit They Were Wrong

Due to how some individuals view broken relationships or marriages, a person in a bad relationship may not want to leave to avoid being blamed. Some individuals believe it's better to be in toxic relationships than leaving because of what people will say. This reasoning is hard to change in the victim, since it has been ingrained in them for a while. Unfortunately, people with this belief often find themselves in the same situation again.

They Don't Want to Make Their Parents Disappointed

Some people are in toxic relationships just to avoid disappointing their parents. But, seeking approval for your happiness and wellbeing from anyone shows you have low self-esteem. No one is perfect, and if your parents blame you for leaving a bad relationship, then they do not understand or love you enough. It's up to you to make them see the reasons why you left. No matter what happens to your relationship, you shouldn't bother about what others think. Instead, you should work on being a better you and have a high level of confidence in yourself and your ability. Seeking validation from others shows you do not love and respect yourself.

They have Lost Hope

Being abused and tortured emotionally and physically for an extended period can be damaging. Due to this, people in bad relationships do not believe they can find love again. The toxicity of their partner has eaten deep into their mind, body, and soul that they do not have

belief in themselves. They give up on their dreams and life with the belief that there's no perfect life anywhere. With these thoughts and many others, they become hopeless of a brighter future and endure the pain they consistently get in their toxic relationship.

They Feel Guilty

Abusive people tend to manipulate others into believing that they are the reasons for their behavior or everything wrong in the relationship. They always play the victim and will blame you for their abusive actions. They tell you how undeserving you are of people like them and what you've put them through by your nagging and complaining. You can never win them because they know your weaknesses and will use it against you. With time, you'll start believing their words, and feeling of guilt starts to creep in.

When you continuously get blamed for what happens whenever you talk to your partner, you gradually lose your self-esteem and feel guilty. When this happens consistently, having a reasonable discussion with your abusive partner becomes difficult. So, if you find yourself in such a situation, the best thing to do is to leave. Being abusive is what it is, and nothing can justify such action. Even when you get blamed for being abused, understand it's not your fault and leave before it becomes messier.

They are Scared of Being Alone

Many people in bad relationships dread being alone because they've come to depend totally on their abusive partner for support and happiness. They believe being with their toxic partner is a pleasure and an opportunity that many wish to have and as such, they'll prefer staying. But what is wrong with being alone and enjoying your company? Absolutely nothing! In fact, being alone at such times is necessary for self-rediscovery and improvement. You'll get to discover your passion and hidden potentials and work more on being a better version of yourself. It's also a great time to meditate on your life's journey and discover how to identify a toxic relationship from miles away. With this, you'll be able to move on to happier and healthier relationships since you now know what you want.

Chapter 7: How to Help the Partner to Engage in the Relationship More Serenely

In healthy relationships, there are instances where all seems fine, and the couple shares a deep connection. In other cases, the connection seems off. There are also moments when individuals in a relationship want different things at a specific point in time. Toxic relationships tend to grow as a result of situations like these. For most toxic relationships, it is still possible to bring it back into the lines of a healthy one. However, this is only applicable to toxic relationships without severe emotional abuse or physical abuse. If there is an abuse of any form in the relationship, there is no point sticking around as many abusers never change. For your own safety, and that of your kids, if any, the best step for you here is to leave.

The reality is that saving a relationship or getting your partner on the right path to a healthy relationship only works if they are willing. If the other partner refuses to get past the situation at hand, then you would be unable to make your relationship better again no matter how hard you try. If you can find out the reason for the distance between you and your partner in a relationship, you are well on your way to ensuring more serenity in the relationship. In this chapter, we will be elaborating on how you can do just this and bring your partner towards the direction of a healthy relationship.

Point Out What Is Triggering the Problem

The first step to correcting a toxic relationship is to determine what is bringing about the problems in the first place. It is essential for you and your partner to work together to determine this. Here, you both can speak about what is bothering you and think of ways to sort them out. Could the problem be as a result of trust issues? Problem with insecurity? Or issues with control among others? Regardless of what is bringing about the issue, it is essential that you determine what it is to allow you to come up with ways to fix them.

Ensure You Have the Correct Disposition

Determining what is triggering the problem in your relationship will not get you anywhere if you both do not have the right attitude or temperament. You and your partner should both be willing to get rid of the issues that are bringing about an unhealthy relationship. At this point, you both should be prepared to go all out to sort it out rather than coming up with excuses. Correcting problems of any kind requires commitment, and when the issues have to do with a relationship between two people, it can be even more difficult. If both of you are not on the same page at this point, then you won't be able to get past this step.

Clearly Communicate About It

Like we have covered earlier, one of the core foundations for a healthy relationship is communication. Now that you are on the same page with your partner, you need to talk about the problems in the relationships. This conversation should be centered around the problems that are making your relationship unhealthy. When speaking about these problems, you need to keep a level head as being angry won't get you anywhere. You need to be open when portraying your message. You must tell your partner how you feel respectfully and concisely, to make sure they do not get the wrong interpretation of your motives.

When speaking to your partner, do not beat around the bush. You have to go straight to the point. If you call them out in anger, they may go on the defensive. Having a conversation with someone who has been placed on the defensive may not bring about any tangible results. When letting your partner know how you feel, try to consider their own views and perspective too. This will make them place themselves in your story and get a real glimpse of the way you feel. If they begin to get defensive and start to argue, the best course for you is to calmly remind them that you are only letting them know your perspectives and your feelings. The way you feel and see things are not up for argument. Be sure that you clearly state this, because the way you see the relationship is just as meaningful as the way they see it. The goal of the whole conversation is not to argue about the way you feel and your perspective.

During this sort of conversation with your partner, the following are the outcomes that may arise: The partner who is the offender becomes remorseful, or they get upset. If the latter is the case, you need to keep a level head. If you get angry as well, you will only bring yourself down to their level, and an argument will start, which won't get you anywhere. Besides, getting angry will take the conversation off course. If you fall into this trap of anger, the conversation will now be centered about the way they feel instead of the toxic behavior they are exhibiting. Your goal of the conversation is to urge them to ask what areas of their behaviors need improvement. If they do this, you should have a few ideas in mind to tell them instantly.

Also, you and your partner need to develop strategies for communication. You need to ponder in advance what you would both say, especially if you don't feel like you are being treated healthily. You could come up with a safe word of both your choosing to let the other person know that things are escalating. This is a great method of letting your partner know exactly how a particular situation is bothering you. No matter what route you and your partner decide to go with, just agree beforehand the method of communication you both want to employ. Another great strategy would be to choose a period of the day where you both can pour out all of your feelings without any restraints. Just ensure you remain consistent with the option you go with. Every misunderstanding you have needs to be discussed, and nothing should be left pending. This way, you will prevent the possibility of any resentment building up to cause something even worse later on. However, all of these will only work if you are both willing to put the same level of effort.

Establish Mutual Ground

Like we have stated above, the aim of communication with your partner is to let them see things from your perspective. By now, they should understand the behavior they are exhibiting that is bringing about a problem. The instant they can understand where you are coming from, you should also try to understand their perspective as well. Doing this will aid you both into coming up with solutions or compromises that are mutually beneficial to you both. For instance, if you love to head out to parties every other weekend, and your partner tends to feel jealous when you spend time with others at these events, then you both can reach a compromise where you spend time together or head to parties as a couple. This will ensure your partner remains assured and does not feel left out in the relationship. Doing this will let them see that you are willing to do all you can to fix your relationship.

This step is not one which is easy, especially if the relationship is not a new one. Nonetheless, it is a very vital one if you plan on making a relationship healthy again. If you are dating a partner who wants an update on everything you are doing, you can calmly tell them how you appreciate the fact that they care about you. However, it can be a bit tasking sending an update every other minute, especially when you are at work. Let them know they will be the first on your dial list in the event something serious ever takes place. Once you have done this, ask them to consider where you stand.

Don't Ignore Your Flaws

Blaming your partner for all the issues you are facing in your relationship can be quite straightforward. But it does not mean it is right. You need to also look into how you may have contributed to the conflicts currently going on in your relationship. So, you need to take a moment and consider your flaws, accept them, and think of ways you can become a better person. It is essential to let go of pride and admit that you are not a perfect person.

You both are not in a competition, but it is instead a partnership between two individuals. This means you don't need to keep track of who messed up the most. You should work towards recognizing the areas where you are both defaulting in your relationship and do all you can to make it a healthy one filled with love.

Remember the Good Times

As humans, it is effortless to focus on the bad memories as opposed to the good ones. The same applies to relationships as well. When you feel a relationship has become unhealthy, it is easy to place focus on the negative areas of your partner. You start to focus on how manipulative, insensitive, dominating, and frustrating they are. However, you no longer remember how caring, loving, sweet, and faithful they once were to you, or still are. You fell in love with them for these reasons. It is ideal to always look at things from all aspects. Do not place emphasis on their negative attitudes alone.

Don't Forget to Display Affection

When you are in a relationship with someone who is being mean and controlling to you all the time, showing affection to such a person would probably be the last thing on your mind. However, you need to be willing to prove to your partner that you want to fix your relationship and are eager to put in the effort involved. There are many ways you can show affection to trigger the spark once more. You can go on a couples retreat or on a date to your favorite restaurant. You can also try out new activities structured for couples. This way, you will be able to find out things that you previously did not know about one another. In return, you will be able to see your partner from a new perspective and perhaps bring in the spark once more.

Ensure You Spend Time by Yourself

Spending some alone time is essential under normal circumstances. However, it is even more vital when you are in an unhealthy relationship. By taking some time out and spending time with yourself, you will be able to ponder things and clear up your mind. You need to pay attention to the things that bring you joy and satisfaction. Toxic relationships can be consuming if you let them, so you have to take all the necessary time out to prevent it from overwhelming you. When you take some time alone and get your mind organized, you better prepare yourself to deal with the problem at hand to change the toxic relationship into a healthy one.

Set Longstanding Goals Together

Even if your relationship is presently having issues due to unhealthy behaviors, you should note that these issues get you prepared for future problems. For this reason, you have to let each other understand that this problem is something that will pass soon. If you still both see yourselves having a future together, be sure you do all within your power to fix the relationship so it's healthy again.

Reach out to Your Support System

As a rule of thumb, it is not advisable to bring in a non-professional, third party into your relationship. However, this could be one of your only options when trying to correct the problems you are dealing with in a toxic relationship. Contacting a friend whom you believe is not going to take sides can offer you a non-biased perspective of your relationship. A friend can help remind you of the reasons why your relationship is worth saving.

Before reaching out to your friend, you need to tell them in a detailed manner the kind of help you require from them. You don't want to call on friends who are just going to side with you even when you are wrong, especially if your goal is to fix the relationship. Don't call on friends that would make matters worse. You have to ensure they are completely aware that you are making efforts to fix your unhealthy relationships. For this reason, they do not have to take sides or hurl insults at your toxic partner all through the process of offering their perspective. It is understandable for your friends to take your side and defend you if the need arises. However, in a situation like this, it would only worsen the issues you are trying so desperately to solve.

In playing the role of a support system, your friends should be available to go on outings with you. This would give you an avenue to pour out your thoughts to them, so they let you know what they think. In addition, you could request that they keep communication lines open with you, so they can make sure you are doing fine. The reason for this is simple; many toxic partners tend to isolate the victim, and the situation is even worse when you are vehemently trying to fix the relationship.

Also, note that many of the people close to you may not be willing to offer you support. This is because lots of individuals may not understand why you are even staying in the relationship when the ideal option would be to leave. It is understandable for many of them to leave you to your issues when they are tired of telling you to leave. Nonetheless, you don't need to take it personally as friends tend to say things like that because they love you and care about your well-being. Remember to call on them for support and tell them how you would want them to support you.

Reach Out to A Professional

For many individuals, this is the last resort and can feel like a scary and shameful option. However, you should understand that there is nothing embarrassing about seeking help from experts. You can talk with a therapist, counselor, psychologist, or even a helpline. When you get a perspective from someone outside of your relationship, there are things you would learn about your problem that you would not have seen yourself. Experts do not have any stake in your relationship and would be fair when offering you solutions. This is not the same as your loved ones or friends who may be supportive of one partner over the other. Relationships on their own are not easy, and with toxic behavior, it becomes even more difficult. Getting directions from an external voice who offers logical plans and solutions can be very refreshing. Experts have the needed experience to provide you with solutions that work.

If you feel that the toxicity in your relationship is one that can be solved, then try to convince your partner to get the help of a therapist. However, if your partner has a mindset that is aggrieved or toxic, you may be unable to do anything to get them to seek help. You can try to urge them to get the help of a professional if they want to save your relationship. If needed, you can issue an ultimatum to your partner to save your relationship and follow it through it if they still refuse to seek help. If they agree to therapy, make sure they follow through. Often, people will promise therapy but not follow through with it.

Your partner may not be the only one who requires help in the relationship. You, as the victim of the toxicity, may need help too. There is a high possibility that since you have been dealing with a toxic or abusive relationship, you have picked up a few unhealthy mechanisms for coping. These unhealthy habits, in addition to causing harm to you in the long run, may also be a danger to your partner. This is a situation that could you could deal with by calling on a counselor.

Lastly, you need to bear in mind that for a partner who is extremely manipulative, therapy may not work. This sort of partner could use it to pretend that they have heard your grievances and are willing to work on them. They may act like they are ready to begin a relationship which is free of toxicity with you. However, it is at this moment that these partners may dominate you using all you have poured out. Also, when speaking with the counselor and verbalizing their feelings, they may capitalize on manipulative statements to make you feel like you are the problem.

Fix Your Relationship or Not?

To fix your toxic relationship or not? This decision lies solely on you. There is no right or wrong answer to this, and it depends on the individual in the situation. Your decisions should not be influenced by your partner or the people you know. It should be your decision to make. All of the individuals and support system you call on are only there to help you through your decision. However, you don't have to remain in a relationship because of the amount of time you have invested in it. There is no harm is starting again, as it is a better option than remaining in a relationship with a partner who does not want things to get better.

If you choose to correct the issues in your toxic relationship, your reason should be because of how much you care about your partner. It should also be because your partner is willing to put in the work as well. Trying to fix a toxic relationship because you are scared of starting anew or scared of being judged, is not a wise choice. It is a better idea to start your life again than to keep channeling your efforts and time into a relationship that won't improve.

You also have to note that the harsh truth is that some toxic relationships can't be fixed. In fact, there are toxic relationships you should not try to repair, especially those with constant physical abuse. The reason for this is that many abusers hardly ever change. In time, they revert to their former habits. Also, there are instances where you do all you can to make a relationship work out, and you still end up making no progress. In situations like these, the best step to take would be to leave the relationship and try to get the pieces of your life back together. Nonetheless, if you do feel a relationship could be worth saving, its ideal to at least try to save the relationship first.

Chapter 8: Recognize When Nothing Else Can Be Done

Every individual makes use of psychophysical energies to create an apparent suffering state. The "let's just try to wait it out" mindset comes to mind. Basically, we tend to wait and see what happens with the hope that things will get better in the future. By choosing to stay, we're choosing to create our own state of suffering. This happens when a partner is unwilling to change, and we hesitate to leave.

Anyone who claims that being in a relationship is easy is either lying or delusional. Even the most successful couples will state that there is a lot of work done behind the scenes. The reason why relationships appear to be an easy feat is that the majority of the work is done behind the scenes, the public eye never gets to see just how both parties compromise, sacrifice, or commit to each other. All everyone sees is the united front that both parties have due to the work they have put in. One thing to always remember when venturing into a relationship is that your partner is not responsible for your happiness; they are supposed to add to it. The baseline happiness that any individual in a relationship brings is one that comes from within. So, when do you recognize that nothing else can be done and realize it's time to move on? This is what we will be covering in this chapter.

Your Partner Hurts You Constantly

An indicator that the relationship you are in is not for you is if your partner is a continual source of hurt feelings, resentment, or stress. If you are going through something like this, it might be essential to assess if your relationship is one that is past its date. Every individual has a list of things that would be classified as a no-no in a relationship, with abusive behavior being top of the list. However, in a relationship, there are usually other issues that arise. Most of them can be sorted with a mix of commitment, time, and the help of a therapist. Nevertheless, if you have tried all you can and nothing seems to get better, or it appears that you are the only individual willing to make an effort, it might be necessary for you to move on.

It's Time to Move on if You Are Emotionally or Physically Abused

Physical abuse is one of the things that should never exist in a relationship. However, there are, unfortunately, relationships in which one partner physically abuses the other. There are numerous levels to this; it could be anything from shoving or grabbing to hitting and pushing you. If you are in this type of relationship, it is best for you to leave. This is not a situation you should be in or behavior that can be changed for the better. Is your partner emotionally abusing you or gaslighting you? If you have a partner that informs you that any abusive behavior exhibited by them is simply a product of your imagination, or that you are unnecessarily sensitive, then you should leave.

If You Are in A Relationship That Causes More Harm Than Happiness to You

Regardless of how much love you have for your partner or how you work extra hard to make your connection stronger, it is impossible for you to do it by yourself. When having a partner that seems to be more absent or they are unable to see how their behavior harms you, that is a relationship you should not be in.

It is imperative that you never stick with someone that tends to ask for way more than they provide when it comes to happiness. When you consider everything, there is only a limited amount of time you get to spend alive; it should be spent on things and people that bring joy to our lives. We should experience life with those individuals that want to see to our happiness.

They Seem to Have No Love for You

If we are honest, there is no such thing as two different people in a relationship loving the same way; it just isn't possible. Many individuals believe that the way we interact with others, especially in love, is shaped by our experiences. No two people have ever had the same set of experiences growing up, not even identical siblings. This is why you should dispel the notion or expectation of being loved by your partner the way you love them.

Every individual has their own unique, loving methods. There are times when love becomes unrequited, and even if it is returned, two individuals can't feel the same amount of love. This also means that as with every other feeling, love is not something that can be quantified or measured. When you think about it, everyone should be able to know if their love for someone is unrequited.

There are cases where things are usually glaringly evident, and the love you have for someone is for naught. They either refuse to be with you, or they could choose to use you, but reject the notion of any type of commitment. In many other scenarios, it can be difficult for the truth to be spotted. This could be because they might choose to pretend to love you in the hopes of gaining one type of benefit. It could also be that they were initially infatuated with you but are now confused about how they feel about you. Routine and personal history tend to play an integral role when someone isn't in love with their partner.

Your Partner Refuses to Change

It is okay for people to make mistakes, as there are no perfect humans. However, if you call out your partner for these mistakes and he or she refuses to change, then it becomes a problem. If you inform your partner about how their toxic behavior affects your well-being, and they instead categorize you as over-sensitive or irrational and even blame you for the problems instead, then this is a relationship that can't be saved. At this point, it may be time to leave.

For a relationship to work ultimately, you need a partner that has the same desire to make it work. It is possible to fix even extreme relationships if both partners are ready to do what is needed. However, if your partner refuses to see things from your perspective and bluntly refuses to change, then you need to realize that nothing else can be done. Your only option will be to leave the relationship for your sake.

Chapter 9: Say Enough

There comes a point in time when you need to cease thinking about what you are losing and begin to think about what you will get by leaving the relationship. This is because, the longer you stay in the relationship, the harder it will be for you to get your serenity.

If life was similar to romance movies, the one we fall in love with would be the one to make us happy. However, in reality, things tend to go differently. We fall in love, let our guard down, and someone takes advantage of this to hurt us multiple times. Yes, it is fine to fight for a relationship, but when the relationship is a toxic one, you need to learn when to say enough. This is because if you don't, the damage it will cause you down the line can be irreversible.

Love can seem like an addiction, and like all addictions, there are healthy and unhealthy ones. Relationships, as we have covered in earlier chapters, are also the same. And harmful relationship addictions can break down a person in the most negative ways. A relationship that is toxic and filled with emotional abuse, hostility, danger to you, and other toxic behaviors, are the most difficult to leave. In theory, they should be easy to walk away from, but practically, this is not the case. And this is why it is essential for you to walk away as fast as possible, because the longer you stay, the harder it is to let go.

Knowing When to Say Enough and Walk Away

There are instances when the signs are apparent. These could range from cheating, physical, and emotional abuse, continuous criticism, among others. Sometimes the signs may be as mild as lack of intimacy, perpetual heartache, and loneliness.

It is hard to leave any relationship, including toxic ones. It requires a tremendous amount of strength and energy to say enough and let go of a toxic relationship. So, what do you need to do to help you through the process of saying enough? The steps we will be covering in this section can be of help.

Stay in the Present

It is tempting to live in the memories of your relationship. For instance, how the relationship used to be. The same applies to living in the future. That is hoping that things in your relationship will get a lot better or fantastic. However, if you need to find the strength to leave a toxic relationship, you need to live in the now or present. To do this, experience the entire relationship for what it is at that moment. Doing this will help you see how damaged or toxic the relationship you are trying to save is.

When you constantly look at the relationship the way it once was or the way you hope it would be, to convince yourself to stay, then there is a problem. See the relationship for what it is presently, and it will be less complicated for you to make your choice.

Have a Record

Keeping track of how the relationship makes you feel can be another excellent means of helping you decide. Keep a journal which comprehensively states everything you feel in the relationship. You need to include the day to day events of the relationship over a specific period. If you don't enjoy writing, it is also possible to take advantage of pictures to help you with this. Take a photograph of every vital moment in a relationship that brought out either a bad or good reaction from you. Do it for a specific period which could be 1-2 months, or weeks, depending on what is suitable for you.

After the set period, go through your records and answer the following questions:

- Are the feelings mostly good or bad?
- How often do these feelings take place?
- Is there a pattern?
- Is it a continuous or rare occasion?
- Do you love the person you have become?

If you used pictures:

- Do you look happy or lively or drained out in them?
- Do you seem sadder than usual?

Providing answers to these questions can let you view the relationship the way it is. Without the excuses and paddings, you use to make it more appealing to yourself. In the end, you will see things with more clarity and make the right decision.

Observe What Your Body Says

The mind and the body are interconnected. The connection they both share is one that is quite powerful. If you block off the messages and signs that your mind or gut tries to tell you, then your body takes up the role. You will observe some feelings and signs in your body like tension and heaviness, among others. Also, the way it works will change.

To determine what your body is saying, ask yourself the following:

- Do I feel physical pain in my body?
- Is there a feeling of heaviness in my body?
- Does my body ache?
- Does it look like I am losing weight?

Providing accurate answers to these can help you see the relationship for what it is.

What Is Your Coping Mechanism?

Look within yourself; do you have any coping mechanisms to ensure you don't feel terrible? Or what behaviors have you adopted to help you in the relationship?

As opposed to not dealing with the terrible feelings that arise, try to examine them. When you deal with the pain you are feeling; you will get the strength, bravery, and wisdom you require to be able to say enough.

Put A Deadline in Place

When you hope something to improve in the future, it is not difficult to forget how long you have been waiting. To place a deadline, select a specific period, be it a few weeks, months, or even a day. You need to pick a deadline that you feel is ideal for you. During this period, do all you can for your relationship. Put in as much energy as you can into it until you exceed the period you have set aside for yourself. Then observe the results, and you will find the answer you need.

Get Out of Your Role

In all relationships, each partner picks up a role over time. This is more like a pattern which keeps the relationship going and allows each partner to maintain their behavior. This does not imply that you are responsible for being treated the way you are being treated, especially if the relationship is one that is toxic. However, it does mean that you have picked up a particular way of behaving that makes it easy for you to bear the unhealthy relationship.

In toxic relationships, there is a victim, and there is an abuser. You need to determine what your exact role is. Are you the rescuer? Or the one who keeps giving excuses for the other? Determine your role and try to get out of it. By changing the dynamic this way, it will ensure the unhealthiness in your relationship is more apparent, making it less complicated for you to say enough, and leave the relationship. At the very least, you may trigger a positive change in your partner.

Leave the Imagination Behind

When you fantasize about the possibilities of the future, it can result in you being tied down to a relationship which is toxic. Holding on to fantasies will prevent you from seeing things as they really are. Because you believe things can get much better, as you have seen in your fantasies, you will keep trying until you can try no more.

The more you allow your imagination to rule you, the more you try to change your reality to match your fantasy. The same applies even if you are in an unhealthy relationship. Your imagination will push you to hold on longer than you usually should, even if the relationship is a toxic one. If the way you imagined your relationship was going to become a reality, it would have changed already. So, let go of the imagination, and you will see things for how they are, which in turn will give you the energy to say enough.

Defend your Well-being

By prioritizing yourself, you will indirectly give yourself the energy to fight for you. Everyone, including you, deserve happiness, but in most instances, you will have to fight for the joy you actually want. Give yourself a priority and fight to get the best treatment for yourself in a relationship. When you observe it is not something your existing relationship will offer you, you will get enough energy to walk away.

Stop the Excuses

It is perfectly normal for us as humans to give excuses for those we love. This becomes particularly heightened when we are in a relationship with that person. However, doing this excessively does not make one see the relationship for what it is and can make you stay longer than you should in a toxic relationship.

Search within yourself. Have you ever gotten what you desired from this relationship? How does your desire differ from what you presently have? Does it feel like you are being loved or treated right?

In a healthy relationship, even when arguments arise and we say and do things out of anger, you can still feel the respect and love behind it even during the hard times. Once you stop making excuses for your partner, you will be able to see the relationship more clearly and see it for what it is.

Unhinge Your Mind

If in your mind, you genuinely believe you can't leave, then it will be difficult for you to do so. Do not limit yourself by constantly believing that you can't leave. Change your mindset and tell yourself you can leave when you want to. Make your choices based on what you want, not based on what you think you can't do. By changing your mindset, you will get the strength you desire to make a decision that you truly want.

Take Courage and Make a Decision

Lastly, take courage and make your decision. And whatever you choose to do, ensure you own the choice you make, knowing you were responsible for making this decision. If you don't make a decision now, it may seem fine for a while; however, over time, it will keep you tied down, and without the strength you require to say enough and leave this toxic relationship.

Besides, note that if a relationship feels toxic and unhealthy for you, then it probably is. At this point, you can fight as hard as you can to fix your relationship. However, when you have no more energy to keep on fighting, you will see things clearly, as they are.

Every relationship goes through difficult times and can get past it.

However, in unhealthy relationships, this cycle is repetitive, which makes it essential to either fix it, or leave as soon as you can. The decision to remain or leave an unhealthy relationship lies with you, but you need to be sure your reasons are the right ones when you do make a choice.

If you do decide to say enough and leave the relationship, you will need to learn the appropriate way to do so. The next chapter will break down a few tips that can make this process a seamless one.

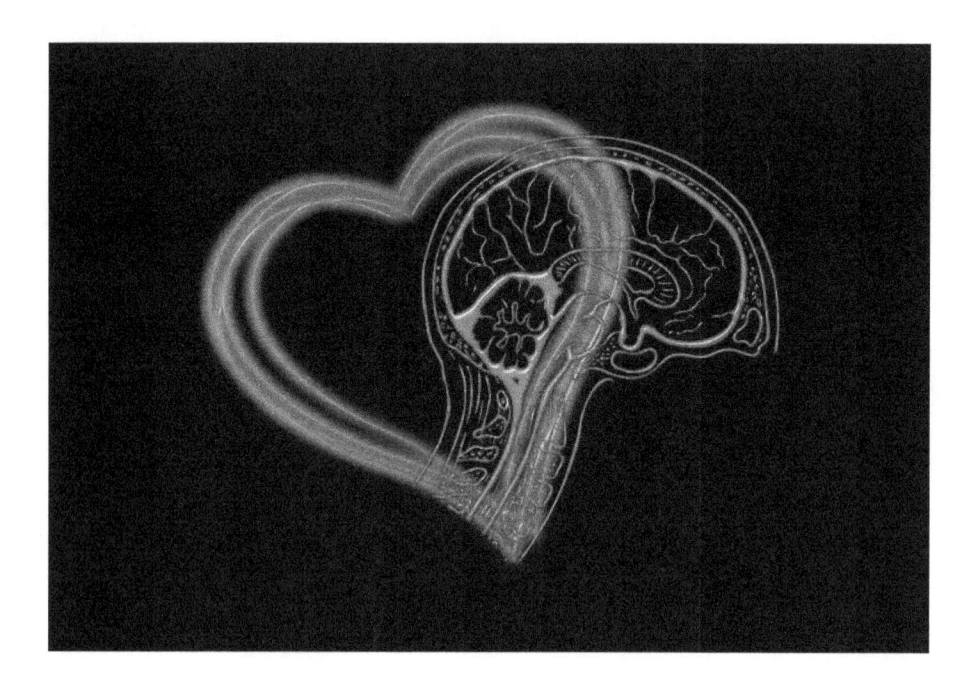

Chapter 10: Tips for Getting Out of a Toxic Relationship

Toxic or not, a long-term relationship can be complicated to leave. You've come to share a lot with your partner, and you just don't know how to leave without remembering the good times you had together. You've lived and eaten together; you've shared your thoughts with this person, and you complement each other. So, it becomes difficult to move away from someone that was an essential part of your life.

On the other hand, toxicity makes it even more difficult to leave even though it should seem easier. The reason is simple for many individuals. They have tried leaving on many occasions, but their toxic partners constantly remind them of how ungrateful and difficult they are. They have concluded that they are not worth being loved and always fear loneliness. Besides, they are utterly dependent on their partner. Many of these individuals have lost their self-esteem, and no matter how much they try, the thought of leaving causes disorientation. They are hell-bent on making it work.

These thoughts, and many of the reasons we have discussed in earlier chapters, are some of the common things that influence people to stay too long in toxic relationships. How then can you know when you're truly ready to leave? The best time to go is when you've identified the problem and built up your self-esteem. If you're not sure of your decisions and you're still battling with fear, leaving becomes difficult. By the time you have your self-esteem back, you'll be able to know what's best for you and understand that you deserve better. At this time, you're entirely ready to move on to healthier relationships.

Are you thinking of leaving finally? If you are, take the steps below, and we hope that you find a healthier and happier relationship in the future. But before then, there are a few things about leaving a toxic relationship you need to know.

Things You Should Know About Leaving a Toxic Relationship

Before you take the decisive step of leaving a toxic relationship, there are a few things you need to know. Knowing them will ensure the breakup process is much easier for you, so you are not caught unawares.

It takes Time for the Damage to Heal

If you've been in a toxic relationship for too long, it can be tough for you to love yourself. Due to the consistent emotional and physical abuse you've been through, you believe you're at fault and hate yourself for this. Your partner may have told you why you need help, maybe saying that you're emotionally unstable and crazy. After hearing it for so long, you believe this with time. This may have taken away your self-worth, and no matter what you do, you'll always remember these things. In the end, when you're ready to move on and let go, you'll begin to love yourself and gradually forget about them.

You May Want to Go Back

Toxic partners are excellent manipulators. They know your weaknesses and what you want. They'll ensure that they make you think about them wherever you are by treating you with love and kindness at the beginning of your relationship. Even if you have left them for a while, you still remember the romantic moments you shared, and you're tempted to going back. And even worse, you may feel ashamed for feeling this way. Nonetheless, you have to know that it's okay to feel this way, but if you give it time, you'll heal completely.

The Choice can Come from Anywhere

It can be tough to spot unhealthy behaviors in your relationship after spending years in it. For this reason, you may not be the one to trigger the decision to break up. Your friends and loved ones are likely not going to be happy seeing you suffer, and they may make a choice for you, but you're not sure it's right. You may not understand what others are seeing because you're blindfolded with love.

Even in a situation when you are getting prepared to end the relationship, you may believe that the other individuals in your life are being too dramatic or blowing things out of proportion. You may also see the truth in what they are trying to tell you. However, with continuous pressure from them, you may end up making the decision to leave anyway. The decision to leave can be triggered from any location. This is not important. What is essential is the fact that you do make the decision.

You May Not Understand What's Normal for Some Time

Due to the kind of environment you have grown accustomed to in your toxic relationship, you will believe that arguments and violence are a normal part of a relationship. You only get to understand what normal behavior is when you talk to your family, friends, and therapist. This process may take time, but eventually, you will understand. Toxic individuals continuously try to teach you the wrong definition of what is normal, but having the right set of people in your life can show you what normal really is.

You May End Up in A Toxic Relationship Again

Leaving a toxic relationship and ending up in another can be very devastating. But there is a high chance that it will happen. There are numerous toxic individuals in this world, and you may come across one or more of them as you try to move on. In our quest to find happiness again, we should try as much as we can to heal completely and recognize toxic behaviors to prevent the repetition of events. This is because the individuals who tend to fall into toxic relationships again after leaving one are those who don't take time to learn, readjust, and recover after dealing with a toxic relationship. When we truly understand what toxicity means and what we should expect from healthy relationships, then we know how to avoid them.

Also, as we have stated earlier, getting the same treatment continuously makes you get used to being treated in that manner. In essence, you may have gotten used to unhealthy partners and come to embrace toxicity and love it. So, it is easier to get into toxic relationships more often, but soon, with continuous efforts, you will get to meet a non-toxic partner who will ensure your happiness.

There can be Danger Associated with Toxic Relationships when Leaving

Any partner that can abuse you emotionally can get physical, even if this is not usually the case. Some toxic partners are good at emotional abuse, while some can go as far as being physically violent. Some may have a weapon at their disposal and react terrifying whenever you want to leave. You need to be watchful and be smart. If a violent, toxic partner finds out you want to break up with them, they may lose it and try to cause you harm.

So, keep yourself safe by seeking out help if you can. Do this by letting your friends and family know before you take a step, or call the police. And if you know you are dealing with an extraordinarily violent partner, break up in an open environment and walk away forever. Regardless of the option you choose to go with, ensure your safety is a priority when trying to leave.

Leaving May Be the Best Decision for You

Leaving a toxic relationship can change your life completely. You'll have the opportunity to work on being a better you and discover your passion. You're able to live a life of peace, happiness, and love. Even though you'll feel the pain sometimes, it's only a part of your healing process, and you'll get past it.

In fact, you may not appreciate the fact that you left the toxic life behind until years after you left. By this time, you're able to find love again, and you're unstoppable.

People May Not Understand Your Decision

A toxic relationship is complicated to explain to people who haven't experienced it before. These people will not understand why you leave and will not support it. And in worse instances, manipulative toxic partners understand how to make themselves look good in the eyes of outsiders, especially friends and loved ones. For many people, your relationship is a perfect one which everyone idealizes. This makes it understandable why many won't understand your reasons for leaving.

Tell them everything without leaving anything out. If they aren't ready to listen, leave them with the hope that they will understand your reason for leaving years later. Remember that you are the one who knows where it hurts, so you need to think about yourself and your sanity first before anyone else's.

Leaving a Toxic Partner Makes You Feel Good

You will experience an aura of freshness that comes with leaving toxicity. Never would you have to watch your steps because you are scared of making your partner angry. You will be free from all the bullying and name-calling. You will also be able to do anything you want without fear of judgment from the one you love. Just feel good and be happy! Close your eyes and embrace the feeling of the freshness of the air. You deserve to be happy, so you should be.

Now that you understand some of the difficulties you may face; let us break down the steps involved in leaving a toxic relationship for good.

Leaving a Toxic Relationship

Practical steps for Leaving a Toxic Relationship

Leaving a toxic relationship is not easy, and if you happen to be in one, remember that it is not your fault. However, as we have earlier stated, it is possible to leave, and the benefits that come along with leaving are enormous. You get to enjoy a life of freedom according to your rules, in an environment without manipulation and abuse.

There are a few practical steps you need to put in place beforehand, to make the process of leaving less complicated and more secure.

- **Put a Safety Plan in Place:** When leaving a toxic relationship, especially those with abuse, it is ideal to plan for your safety. This becomes essential because you never can tell how a scorned toxic partner might react when you leave. Many of them are not predictable, and even if you feel like it is not a necessity, this is something that you should not overlook. For many victims of toxic relationships, one of the most dangerous periods is when they choose to leave. Let your safety be your priority. Create a plan with a professional or someone close to you.

- **Arrange for A Private and Secure Place to Reside:** This is still a part of staying safe. You need a secure location which is unknown by your toxic partner to stay. It becomes even more necessary if there are kids in the equation. The location could be with a loved one, friend, or a shelter for domestic violence. To ensure your chosen location stays confidential, its best to keep your plans to yourself and just a few trust-worthy family members. In a bid to help, lots of loved ones who have your best interest in mind may unknowingly divulge this information to your toxic partner. Many may not understand how serious the issue may be, and may try to fix it in their way. In the end, the results are more detrimental as opposed to positive.

- **Keep a Record of Everything:** Many toxic partners try to reach out to their victims in a bid to get them back. In the process, they may resort to threats, abuse, and manipulation. All of these are done in an attempt to get their partners back. Do all you can to restrict the way you communicate with your ex-partner after you have left. Ensure you keep a record of all the conversations you have with these partners. Take note of the time and dates. All of these will be vital if you ever get into a custody battle for your kids, which is a strategy commonly used by many toxic partners.

- **File for a Restraining Order if Required**: This is not a perfect option; however, they can deter many toxic partners, especially physical abusers. It is also a great way to have the experiences you have had with your toxic partner on record. This kind of record can be useful if the matter does head to court.

- **Get Help with Childcare if There are Kids Involved**: Uprooting your life with kids can be difficult. However, having support can be a huge benefit. Regardless of whether you get help from a friend, babysitter or daycare, ensure there is always someone you can call on in the event of an emergency. There may be things that might require your attention, which may be impossible to attend to if you are the only one looking after your kids.

Getting your Finances in Order

A strategy commonly used by many toxic partners is to abuse their victims financially. They are quick to close shared accounts or ensure the victim has no access to funds if the need arises. This ensures that the victim is directly under their control. Due to this, it becomes crucial to have some form of financial backup away from your partner before you leave.

Below, we will cover a few ways you can achieve this:

- Save and Save Even More: Before you take the step to leave, be sure that you have some funds in your account. This account should be solely in your name and not in a joint account with your partner. Also, it can be helpful to get some credit cards that belong to you alone. All of these can come in handy if you need to leave in a hurry.

If you can, access to a loan. It is an excellent option because your partner does not need to know about it or have access to it. You can get loans from family, friends, and other secure sources. Also, look out for other means of making cash that your partner will have no access or information about.

Better still, if you have a paying job, you can reach out to your HR department to send a portion of your paycheck automatically to another account. It is also possible for your HR to help you alter your W-4, so you can get more cash that is invested or saved all year with every paycheck. There are numerous ways to get the money you can save, and all you need to do is look for an option that suits you best.

- Make Copies of Vital Documents: Make copies of all documents related to your finance that you can lay your hands across. These could range from your vehicle titles, bank statements, tax returns, loan information, and investment statements, among others. You can use a scanner to make virtual copies and save them on the cloud or Google drive. Ensure you do this in a drive that only you have access to. This way, you can get copies of these documents anywhere in the world you decide to go.

- Create a New Bank Account: Open a new bank account that your partner is not aware of. To do this, you will require a new email and mailing address which your toxic partner has no information about. If your partner knows your previous account and has access to it, a great option will be to reach out to your bank and alter your security questions. It is possible to use a question only you know the answer to, and doing this will make sure that only you have access to this account.

Furthermore, take out all of your private items from any deposit box you both used jointly. Head to another bank and make a deposit box of your own. Here, you can place every vital document and valuable which can come in handy later on.

- Get the Services of a Financial Advisor: If it is possible to get the help of a licensed financial advisor, who can cater to your services alone and not you and your partner, it may be a great idea. They can encourage you during your downtimes. If you don't have the resources to hire an expert, there are literature and financial classes you can take advantage of at your local library.

Even friends and members of your family who are great at finance can be of assistance. Regardless of where you find yourself, there is most certainly someone who is very experienced in topics around money. This could be your co-worker, family member, or a loved one. Find a way to contact them and get the help you require.

After putting all you require in place, the following are a few more steps that can ensure that leaving your toxic relationship is less complicated:

Think About What Brought You to This Position

One of the first things to do when you're trying to leave an unhealthy relationship is to think deeply of how you got attracted to the person and why you stayed. If you're able to provide an answer to this, you're one step away from leaving this person. This is because you will learn to point out the unhealthy behavior that makes your relationship toxic

If you don't understand this, you may be tempted to go back because you won't understand why your relationship is toxic. Besides, learning to do this can be of benefit to you in the future. You'll be able to identify a toxic relationship without spending too much time in one. Any form of abuse, be it physical, emotional, or sexual should not be tolerated in any relationship because it's perilous. You need to seek help because there are lots of resources available online which you can leverage.

Fall Back on Family and Friends

When you're in situations that are beyond your control, your family and close friends are there for you. This is because they have a higher tendency of having your back when the odds are not in your favor. You can always reach out to them and let them know what's going on. They've got your back and will always want the best for you. Lean on them at this critical moment and ask for advice. If you think it's important, ask them for accommodation.

As a result of the time you've spent in an unhealthy relationship, you may find it hard to pay attention to some toxic behaviors or words that your partner uses on you. Your friends and family will help you see this if you open up to them without covering up for your partner. They'll be frank with you and let you see things the right way.

As soon as you notice some red flags about your relationship, talk about it to a friend or family. You can speak to them in private and hear what they say. You may have failed to recognize the signs and looming danger, but your friends will help you see this. However, due to the vital role that family and friends play in our lives and the amount of support they provide us, a toxic partner will try to take you away from your loved ones or ensure you don't see or visit them as often as you should. If you find yourself in this situation, it's hazardous, and you should contact someone you trust immediately. Let them know about your partner's constant abuse and controlling habits. Doing this will make you happy, and you'll feel safe knowing that someone is aware of your partner's gameplay.

Make a Clean Break

Ensure that the break up is as clean as possible. Be assertive and make them understand that they shouldn't be any contact between you. Tell them you will not tolerate being harassed or abused and as such will take legal actions if they try that with you.

Stop feeling guilty or concerned about hurting their feelings. They do not care about your feelings, so why should you care about theirs? Right now, the only person important to you is YOU. Your happiness is more important than anyone's at this stage. So, make it a clean break to prevent them from coming back to you.

When people end unhealthy relationships, they're usually concerned about their safety as the partner may abuse, harass, or even become violent with them. When you make a clean break, the probability of facing such issues becomes difficult. If you think your life is under threat and you aren't so sure about your partner's next line of action, involve the police.

Surround Yourself with Positive People

When you're leaving a toxic relationship, do not move with negative people. Surround yourself with people that want the best for you. Practice self-love to attract people that'll treat you with love and care. Be positive and treat yourself well. Take yourself out on a date, spend time outdoors, exercise, go sightseeing or do something that makes you happy. The time people spend in an unhealthy relationship is usually filled with stress and negativity. Replace these stressful and negative emotions with positive ones.

Do Not Feel Sorry for Yourself

Toxic relationships have the capacity to mess with our minds in the strangest ways, which is why they are so difficult to let go of. For one, you will find yourself feeling some self-pity and the thought of moving on may weigh you down. You will also be full of anxiety and fear of letting go. Even though your relationship is unhealthy, you continuously think about this, and you're so scared of letting go. It's okay to feel this way, but you shouldn't let this last for too long. As soon as these thoughts come to your mind, tell yourself that you're stronger than this and moving on is the best. Moving on will make you happy, and it's the best thing to do.

Talk A Therapist

You might have thought that the best person to talk to is family, but you're not so sure about their sense of judgment, or they just aren't a good option. Thus, the next step is to see a therapist or a third-party professional. Having someone to support you and look at your relationship from the perspective of an outsider is an excellent idea as they may give you cogent reasons why you need to leave. They'll also speak to you frankly without being sentimental. Staying in a toxic relationship can affect your mental and physical health. In a research study carried out in 2014, it was discovered that people in unhealthy relationships have anxiety problems, disturbed sleep, heart problems, and stress.(Medic, Wille & Hemels, 2017)

After leaving a toxic relationship, these issues will always remain for the early part of your break up until you're ready to let go and heal completely. It's just like getting healed from a physical wound.

Be Firm with Your Decision to Leave

Often, we miss people when we leave them, and this is normal. The bad parts of our relationships are usually forgotten while the good parts are mostly remembered. There are even times that we wish the person is still in our lives as we can't deal with their absence. This is why we need to have a deep thought before making our decision.

 You need to be sure that you're ready to do this and try as much as you can to stick to your decision. Always remind yourself of what you stand to gain by leaving and why it's the best option for you. If you find yourself unable to handle it alone, confide in your therapist, a close friend, or family. Let them know all that you're thinking about and why you need them now more than ever. They're there to provide the support you need, but you need to remain firm and stick to your decision.

Don't Forget to Love Yourself

Loving yourself is more important to you at this point, and you shouldn't compromise this for anything. Your happiness should come first in all you do. Sometimes, you don't even have to speak to someone you broke up with again if they aren't worth it. It's your happiness that matters, and you should associate yourself with only what makes you happy.

You can't find love in an unhealthy relationship, so, leaving such a relationship means you love yourself and you're putting yourself first. Sometimes, loving yourself comes from letting go. Instead of holding on to a relationship that clearly isn't working, spend time doing things you love. So, love yourself, and you'll start attracting happier and healthier relationships.

Chapter 11: Why Does Getting Over an Unhealthy Relationship Seem Hard?

Sometimes, getting over a toxic ex may seem complicated, and moving on becomes very hard. One strange thing is that we tend to find it challenging to leave a toxic person and forget about them, but the reverse is also the case when we're leaving a healthy relationship. We move on too quickly without looking back.

Even though you may want to hasten how soon you heal and move on, some factors will always determine how long you spend in a relationship and why you can't get over it and move on. Learning these factors will help you better understand why you are finding it difficult to forget your toxic partner completely. We will be looking into these factors below.

You are Thinking About the Positive Aspects Alone

Toxic partners are good at what they do, and they'll ensure that you have lots of wonderful, beautiful, and loving moments to always remember. When you remember these moments, you'll find it hard to believe that a person with so much love and kindness at the beginning will turn out beastly later. Many toxic partners, especially narcissists, do this as a means of playing on your mind, and you'll become indecisive as you're not sure of what to think. If they were abusive from the onset, you wouldn't have committed yourself in such a relationship.

"Love bombing" is one of the tactics used by many toxic partners, especially narcissists, in the early part of the relationship. You'll be adored and cherished like you're the best thing that ever happened to them. It will be too hard to believe as you're swept off your feet and everything seems to be happening fast. At this point, you're already in love and very convinced that this is your ideal kind of life partner.

As soon as this phase is over, the manipulation, bullying, abuse, and degradation begins. You'll be continuously abused physically or emotionally till you break down completely. At this time, you still find it difficult to believe they're abusive and you look forward to a change after a series of apologies have been tendered. Then comes a series of gifts, outings, or anything to make you happy, accompanied by more apologies and promise to change.

By the time you're trying to put the negativity in the past and move on, another abuse occurs, but this time, worse. These things happen so fast that you forget the bad times quickly but have more memories of the good times. All of these positive aspects make it very difficult for one to get over toxic relationships.

The Breakup Catches You Unawares

The major technique used by toxic partners after they have consistently abused their victim is to end the relationship without warning. For many individuals, this can be devastating and coupled with abuse, the pain is enhanced.

In essence, even though the relationship is toxic and you're often told by your partner that they'll leave you whenever you disagree, a break up can seem abrupt as you're caught unawares. Since you didn't prepare for it, you'll have little or no answers to all your questions. You can't really say why they left or what went wrong, and this can be mentally devastating.

With this, starting a new relationship becomes complicated. You'll blame yourself because you're not sure of what the problem is, as your self-esteem has been severely bruised.

As a result of this, moving on becomes difficult at this point. The more you try to fix the relationship or seek answers to the numerous questions on your mind, the harder and longer it becomes for you to leave. You're lost at this point with messed up thinking, and you need to be strong and be firm to overcome this feeling and totally let go.

You Have Been Blamed for Everything That Went Wrong

Often, you've been blamed for being responsible for how the relationship turned out. This is a technique used by most toxic partners. They blame you for making them abuse you and for ruining the beautiful relationship they're trying to build. As a result of the blame dished out to you by your toxic partner, you start to think of ways you could have done better even after the breakup. Thoughts like these make it challenging to let go as you keep thinking of how you could have done better to prevent the abuse.

However, this pattern of thinking isn't correct, and you need to get rid of it. The reality is that you can't stop someone from being dominating, manipulative, or hurtful. But thinking that you can do this, results in you holding on to the relationship longer than necessary. If you really want to get over a toxic relationship, you need to let go of this thought pattern.

You Isolated Yourself from Friends and Family While You Were Dating

A toxic person knows they're toxic and they'll do everything to ensure you don't find out. They are aware that when you tell your friends about their behavior, they'll likely point out that you're in an unhealthy relationship. So, they ensure that you do not make new friends or visit your closest friends. In fact, a toxic person can move with you to a very far place, away from family and friends. With this, your social life is affected negatively, and your life completely revolves around them.

Moving on will become easier when you reunite with your friends and family and let it all out. Your close friends will always want the best for you and leaning on them in times like this will help you heal faster. However, ensure that these friends want the best for you, as you can't deal with more negativity at this stage. All you need right now are positive people that can provide the necessary support and care for you.

Sometimes, reuniting may become hard if you just neglected your friends or relocated with your toxic partner without saying a word to them. But, if you apologize and explain all that you've been through, your friends will be more than happy to have you back and help you heal quickly.

Your Self-Esteem Is Not as Great as It Used to Be

Toxic partners, particularly narcissists, are very good at breaking down the self-esteem of their victims. This is because they're masters in emotional and physical abuse, degradation, and devaluation. They make you feel like you're worthless and undeserving of good things. Then, you begin to believe all the negative words they've filled you with and you will gradually lose your confidence.

If you're good at something or you enjoy doing something, they'll always come up with a negative aspect of it without caring about your feelings or the happiness you derive from such thing. They complain about the way you dress, the friends you keep, your body, your chosen career, and life goals and you'll be left with no option but to believe you're lucky by being with this person.

This is the same treatment you get when you are in a relationship with individuals like this. Now, even after you have broken up with these individuals, the effect of the abuse you have taken over the years still lingers. Because you believe you are nothing without them, you find it hard to get over the relationship. Once you let go of these limiting beliefs, you will be able to recover your esteem and get over the relationship faster.

You Still Have Trust Issues

At the beginning of a toxic relationship, you have so much trust in this person due to the amount of love they've shown you and how down to earth they seem. As you progress, you discovered it was only a façade, and you couldn't forgive yourself for falling for such a trap. As a result of this, you find it difficult to trust other people that come your way and moving on to a healthier and happier relationship becomes hard.

You need to understand that not everyone will be like your toxic partner. It is fine to exercise some caution going forward, but there are a lot of people that would be worth your trust down the road. Forgive yourself and give yourself the chance to trust once more if your goal is to move on.

Chapter 12: How to Recover from a Toxic Relationship

Coming up with a final decision to leave an unhealthy relationship may come with feelings of guilt, especially when you've spent longer than necessary with a toxic person. Like we have stated numerous times, toxic relationships are the hardest to recover from even after you have broken up. However, the instant you can free yourself from the feelings of self-blame and self-guilt, you'll experience total well-being and happiness.

The recovery phase after the relationship has ended is one of the most challenging stages you will deal with. For many, it is even more difficult than leaving the toxic relationship because of all the abuse they must have endured during the relationship.

For this reason, in this section, we will be delving into a few steps that you need to take if you want to reclaim your self-confidence, dignity, and self-esteem. Below are a few of them.

Detach from Your Toxic Partner Completely

A great move to make after ending a relationship to ensure you heal fast is to stop contacting your former partner. The same is also the case in a toxic relationship. After you have ended the relationship, you need to make sure that you cut all forms of communication with your ex-partner.

Toxic people are very good at manipulation, and if you contact them, you may be tricked into changing your mind and going back to them. Cutting them off is vital because, at this stage, you are still in search of closure and require answers for the things you did wrong. This is the case even when you know you won't get any substantive response. Also, even after the breakup, you will still feel some vulnerability for your former toxic partner. You have to continuously remind yourself of how you got here in the first instance. Do not make yourself available to be abused once more. You need to act like you and your former toxic partner are in different parts of the world. Your ex would do all they can to open the communication lines with you once more. Make sure you block all their phone numbers and make yourself unavailable for them to reach you.

Avoid contacting them through phone calls or social media channels and block them if need be. Disengage entirely from the toxic individual as this will help you heal faster. Ensure you move as far as you can away from them regardless of how difficult it may seem. If you both had kids together, you might need the assistance of an experienced intermediary if you need to contact them. If this is impossible, search for a therapist with the right qualifications to put together a parenting plan for you. This is a legally binding document which consists of all the data about financial obligations and time-sharing for children. It should also include accepted ways for both parties involved to communicate. This will help make the process even more straightforward.

Work Towards Being a Better You

You're free from constantly being pulled down or being told what to do or what not to do. So, you should start learning to work on yourself and let people know the new you through your actions and words. Do only what makes you happy and understand that you should make decisions and do things because of you and not because of anyone else.

Cleanse Your Mind, Body, and Soul of Negativity

A toxic relationship is just like an unhealthy meal. When you eat such a meal, you'll be affected, and your chance of falling ill is very high. So, free your mind, body, and soul of such toxicity. Be positive in every sense of the word by taking part in activities that'll make you happy. You can cleanse your mind by exercising, sightseeing, going out, or being a part of group therapy. If you love singing, writing or dancing, please do so! Just do anything to achieve a mind filled with positivity.

Do Things That'll Boost Your Confidence

Constant belittling and abuse will most likely make you lose your confidence. The more your toxic partner put you down, the more you lose your self-worth and confidence. You've also come to believe you can't do without your partner as they constantly make you feel worthless. To prove to yourself that they've been very wrong about you, you need to build your self-confidence by doing things you're afraid of doing. Are you afraid of public speaking? Why not start by contributing to talk therapy and improve as you gain your confidence back.

Be confident in your decision-making, career goals, and all other things you need to do without looking for validation from anyone. Tell yourself, "I've got this", and do great things that'll surprise you. Most importantly, be confident about your body and yourself and recovering from a toxic relationship will become easier!

Surround Yourself with Positive People

One key feature of a toxic individual is pessimism. While trying to move on from a toxic relationship may be hard, don't make it harder by hanging around negative people. Instead, surround yourself with as much positive energy as possible. You don't want to leave an abusive relationship and get abused again. If this happens, it means you haven't learned from your previous experience. Move with people that are ready to bring out the best in you and support you always. Your friends understand that you're trying to heal and if they love you, they'll help you through this period.

Enjoy Your Own Company

If you don't love yourself, how then will people love you? When you learn to enjoy being alone, you'll discover something new about yourself and love yourself more. Being alone shouldn't amount to loneliness; instead, it should be a time to meditate and reflect on your life and what to do to make yourself happy.

As soon as you're able to understand this, it becomes easy to move on, and you don't have to be scared of being lonely. You will also discover that being alone offers you peace, and you're happier than being with an abusive partner.

Try to Love Again

If you don't want to love again after leaving an abusive partner, it's understandable! Due to your experience with a toxic partner, you may find it hard to love again. But, there's someone out there dying to be with someone like you. You deserve to be loved and should not deny yourself the opportunity of experiencing a healthier and happier relationship. Whenever you're ready to date, ensure that you watch out for signs of toxicity in people you meet to avoid repetition. Be very sure that you're prepared to move on before you decide to do so.

Conclusion

Well done!! You have gotten to the end of the journey. The fact that you read through to the end shows your level of seriousness in freeing yourself from your toxic partner. Surviving a toxic relationship without a few psychological scars is no easy feat. However, you survived! You have your power, and you need to congratulate yourself for that. Also, don't forget that all of the issues you faced in the relationship were not your fault, and no matter what your partner says to you, the blame is not yours to bear.

It takes a sound support system and a considerable level of commitment to break free from a toxic relationship and completely recover. It is not easy to achieve. However, it is not impossible. Reading this book does not mean the process will be automatic. However, it will arm you with the right information to ensure the process of breaking up and recovery is much more comfortable. Read, understand, and implement all you will learn in this book, and with time, you will be on the path to true happiness. I sincerely hope you can attain your desired life.

References

5 Signs You Are in a Toxic Love Relationship. (2017). Retrieved 10 August 2019, from https://medium.com/thrive-global/5-signs-you-are-in-a-toxic-love-relationship-863d61b5b9e3

7 Types of Toxic People and How to Spot Them | Science of People. Retrieved 10 August 2019, from https://www.scienceofpeople.com/toxic-people/

7 Ways to Peacefully End a Toxic Relationship. Retrieved 10 August 2019, from https://www.powerofpositivity.com/7-ways-peacefully-end-toxic-relationship/

Alexis, S. (2015). 5 Signs Your Toxic Relationship Is Not Worth Saving. Retrieved 10 August 2019, from https://thoughtcatalog.com/sabrina-alexis/2015/11/5-signs-your-toxic-relationship-is-not-worth-saving/

Bowlin, Y. 5 Signs You're in a Toxic Relationship. Retrieved 10 August 2019, from https://tinybuddha.com/blog/5-signs-youre-in-a-toxic-relationship/

Brown, L. (2018). Toxic relationship: Don't ignore these 40 warnings signs!. Retrieved 10 August 2019, from https://hackspirit.com/toxic-relationship-signs/

Daskal, L. 35 Signs You're in a Toxic Relationship. Retrieved 10 August 2019, from https://www.inc.com/lolly-daskal/35-signs-youre-in-a-toxic-business-relationship.html

Ducharme, J. (2018). https://time.com. Retrieved 10 August 2019, from https://time.com/5274206/toxic-relationship-signs-help/

Hollis, M. (2015). 13 Signs You're In A Toxic Relationship And It's Ruining Your Life. Retrieved 10 August 2019, from https://www.elitedaily.com/dating/13-signs-youre-toxic-relationship-ruining-life/966801

Intimate partners with low self-esteem stay in unhappy relationships. (2015). Retrieved from https://www.sciencedaily.com/releases/2015/02/150227154826.htm

Katehakis, A. (2018). The Psychology of Addictive Relationships. Retrieved 10 August 2019, from https://psychcentral.com/blog/the-psychology-of-addictive-relationships/

Kennedy, T. How to Leave a Toxic Relationship When You're Still in Love. Retrieved 10 August 2019, from https://tinybuddha.com/blog/how-to-leave-a-toxic-relationship-when-youre-still-in-love/

Kelly, K. (2018). What To Do If You're In An Asymmetrical Relationship. Retrieved 10 August 2019, from https://madamenoire.com/1044532/what-to-do-if-youre-in-an-asymmetrical-relationship/

Medic, G., Wille, M., & Hemels, M. (2017). Short- and long-term health consequences of sleep disruption. *Nature And Science Of Sleep, Volume 9,*

151-161. doi: 10.2147/nss.s134864

Important things no one told you about leaving a toxic relationship. (2018). Retrieved from https://www.yourtango.com/2018315463/10-important-things-no-one-told-you-about-leaving-toxic-relationship

Stanley, S., Rhoades, G., Kelmer, G., Scott, S., Markman, H., & Fincham, F. (2018). Unequally into "Us": Characteristics of Individuals in Asymmetrically Committed Relationships. *Family Process*, *58*(1), 214-231. doi: 10.1111/famp.12397

Toxic Relationships - HealthScope. (2019). Retrieved from https://www.healthscopemag.com/health-scope/toxic-relationships/

Therapy, H. (2016). Addictive Relationships - 15 Signs You Might Be In One - Harley Therapy™ Blog. Retrieved 10 August 2019, from https://www.harleytherapy.co.uk/counselling/addictive-relationships.htm

Young, K. When Someone You Love is Toxic - How to Let Go, Without Guilt -. Retrieved 10 August 2019, from https://www.heysigmund.com/toxic-people-when-someone-you-love-toxic/

Young, K. 15 Signs of a Toxic Relationship -. Retrieved 10 August 2019, from https://www.heysigmund.com/toxic-relationship-15-signs/

CPSIA information can be obtained
at www.ICGtesting.com
Printed in the USA
BVHW041203010321
601386BV00008B/564